# BUILDING

# SUSTAINABLE

# COMMUNITIES

# TOES BOOKS

**The Other Economic Summit (TOES)** is an international forum for the presentation, discussion, and advocacy of the economic ideas and practices upon which a more just and sustainable society can be built -- "an economics as if people mattered."

Those active in TOES are convinced that promising and constructive alternatives are available and are being developed and implemented all over the globe. TOES builds on a considerable tradition of theory and practice. An economics constrained by respect for the natural world and human dignity *is* possible. It is the goal of TOES to promote its further conceptualization and to encourage its elaboration in practice.

TOES books deal with issues on the TOES agenda and seek to further dialogue on and increase understanding of those issues.

TOES/North America is part of an international network of independent but cooperating initiatives working for a more just and sustainable society.

# BUILDING SUSTAINABLE COMMUNITIES

## Tools and Concepts for Self-Reliant Economic Change

Contributors:

C. George Benello
Robert Swann
Shann Turnbull

Edited by Ward Morehouse

A TOES Book

The Bootstrap Press
New York

Published 1989

ISBN 0-942850-11-4

The Bootstrap Press is an imprint of the Intermediate Technology Development Group of North America, Suite 9A, 777 United Nations Plaza, New York, NY 10017.

**Library of Congress Cataloging-in-Publication Data:**

Building sustainable communities : tools and concepts for self-reliant economic change / edited by Ward Morehouse ; contributors, C. George Benello, Robert Swann, Shann Turnbull.
    p.  cm.
    Bibliography: p.
    ISBN 0-942850-11-4
    1. Regional economics. 2. Economic development. 3. Geography, economic. I. Morehouse, Ward. II. Benello, C. George. III. Swann, Robert S. IV. Turnbull, Shann.

HT388.B85 1989
338.9 - dc19                                         88-24123

Cover Design by Noel Malsberg

Printed in the United States of America.

*To the memory of C. George Benello,*
*tireless seeker of a more just working world*

## About This Book

This book is a revised and expanded version of parts of the *Handbook for Community Economic Change*, published in 1983 by the Intermediate Technology Development Group of North America. It is based on the Schumacher Society Seminars on Community Economic Transformation. Further information on the seminars and its other activities may be obtained from the Schumacher Society, Box 76A, Great Barrington, MA 01230 (telephone: 413/528-1737).

## Note to Readers

For further information on the tools and concepts presented here and experience with their application, readers are encouraged to contact the principal contributors directly:

Robert Swann, Schumacher Society, Box 76A, Great Barrington, MA 01230, USA (413/528-1737)

Shann Turnbull, M.A.I. Services, Pty. Ltd., GPO Box 4359, Sidney, NSW 2001, Australia (61-2/233-53450)

In the case of the late George Benello, interested readers are asked to contact the organization in which he himself was active for many years and which is working for many of his principles and ideals:

Industrial Cooperative Association, Suite 203, 58 Day Street, Somerville, MA 02144, USA (617/629-2700)

# CONTENTS

# PREFACE

The original idea for this book came from the First Seminar on Tools for Community Economic Transformation, organized by the E.F. Schumacher Society at Simon's Rock in Western Massachusetts in July 1982, and jointly sponsored by the Society, the Intermediate Technology Development Group of North America, and the Durruti Institute. The purpose of the book is to share more widely the concepts and principles around which this and subsequent Schumacher Society seminars were organized as well as to provide material presented at the seminars in more readily accessible form to others not able to take part.

This book reflects the basic focus of the seminars on "bottom up" rather than "top down" economic transformations. The basic concepts underlying self-reliant community revitalization include community land trusts, various forms of community self-management, and community banking and currency systems that make possible self-financing of community economic change.

*Building Sustainable Communities* is like the process of community economic transformation; it is based on the cooperative effort of many persons. Bob Swann, Shann Turnbull, and the late George Benello who played such key roles in the Schumacher Society seminars in leading the discussion and injecting so many innovative ideas and provocative concepts have played the same role with this book as the principal contributors.

Several persons associated with ITDG have been involved in editorial preparation and production. Judi Rizzi, Vaughan James, and Elinor Tonsing have all labored over drafts of material, transcribing sections of the manuscript and helping in other ways to render it in more coherent form. Vaughan James has undertaken the composition, and Cynthia T. Morehouse has looked after copy editing, proofreading, and production supervision.

My colleague, David Dembo, Program Coordinator at the Council on International and Public Affairs, and two research assistants at the Council, Lucinda Wickle and Jonathan Heller, also helped, especially in tracking down elusive entries for the Bibliography. David Ellerman, Staff Economist and one of the founders of the Industrial Cooperative Association, was also helpful in identifying material on recent developments in the worker cooperative movement.

While all of the persons I have mentioned have played an important role in making the book possible, by far the most important contribution has been made by Bob Swann and Susan Witt of the Schumacher Society. Without Bob's and Susan's determination to make the seminars happen as self-financed, self-reliant exercises in their own right, this book never would have been born.

The first version of this book was published in 1983 and included several case studies based on the application of the concepts presented here. The present version has been revised and updated with new material on conceptual issues but without the case studies. It has also been retitled to reflect these changes.

A word about authorship which is not surprisingly eclectic in a book of this character. Most chapters are ascribed to the three principal contributors and have been drawn from material they originally prepared for the Schumacher Society seminars, typically revised and adapted for publication here. In a few cases, material has been excerpted and adapted from previously published material but significantly revised for inclusion in this book. For example:

- Chapter IV is excerpted and adapted from Robert Swann, "Land, Land Trusts, and Employment," *Green Revolution* (York, Pennsylvania: School of Living, 1977).
- Chapter XI is based on Robert Swann, "The Community Land Trust: An Alternative," Whole Earth Papers, No. 17 (East Orange, New Jersey: Global Education Associates, April 1982).
- Chapter XVI is derived from an article by Shann Turnbull, "The Road to Utopia," *Australian Penthouse*, January 1979.
- Chapter XX has been adapted from Shann Turnbull's book, *Democratising the Wealth of Nations* (Sidney: Company Directors Association of Australia, 1975).

In other cases, the circumstances surrounding preparation and/or publication of material in the book are given in footnotes to chapter titles -- e.g., Chapters XIII and XIV.

In cases where no authorship has been ascribed, the material has been excerpted and adapted from sources in the formulation of which one or more of the principal contributors to this book were involved. The major instance of this character occurs in Chapters V, VI, VII, VIII, and X, all of which are drawn from the Conference Report on Land Trusts, held in Lincoln, Massachusetts in April 1982 and sponsored by the Massachusetts Audubon Society. Another instance occurs in Chapter IX, which is drawn from *Bootstrap Community Revitalization in North America: An Account of the First Seminar on Tools for Community Economic Transformation* (New York: Intermediate Technology Development Group of North America, 1982).

Unfortunately, while work on this version of the book was under way, one of the principal contributors, George Benello, died unexpectedly. His premature passing is a great loss to the search for a more just and equitable world of work, particularly through worker ownership an self-management of which he was a tireless advocate and committed practitioner. *Building Sustainable Communities*, to which he contributed so substantially, is dedicated to his memory.

Finally, it should be emphasized that none of those who have been identified as helping with the preparation of this book is in any way responsible for its shortcomings. As editor, I took it to be my role to give overall shape to the book, even including adaptation of material from the principal contributors so as better to relate to other parts of the book and the overall themes addressed in its pages. Consequently, I must take full responsibility for what follows.

New York
1988

**Ward Morehouse, Chairman**
**Intermediate Technology**
**Development Group**
**of North America**

# INTRODUCTION

INTRODUCTION

# Chapter 1

# THE WORLD CRISIS AND COMMUNITY ECONOMIC REVITALIZATION

*Ward Morehouse*

The world's economy is in a mess. Poverty and income inequality are on the increase and not just in developing countries. Even in relatively affluent economies like the U.S. and Canada, where income inequality steadily declined for a number of decades, it has not reversed course and is growing once again.

Unemployment has become an endemic problem, and again, not just in the Third World countries but in industrialized economies as well. Official unemployment rates mask the true extent of joblessness. In the U.S. and Canada, the jobless rate is twice the unemployment rate, sometimes more, as the number of "discouraged workers" grows. These are persons who have simply given up looking for a job in the organized economy because they cannot find one. Because they have stopped looking they are no longer considered part of the labor force and therefore not even counted as unemployed!

A growing proportion of all the jobless are eking out a living of sorts in the informal economy. No one knows how large that economy is, involving all sorts of barter transactions and off-the-books working arrangements. But it is widely recognized as growing, probably faster than most "mainstream" economists and public officials care to admit.

Current trends in the economies of advanced and industrialized countries like the U.S. and Canada are likely to drive more and more people out of the mainstream economy into the other local, community-based economy.  Most new jobs (three-fourths during the 1980s in the United States) are dead-end service sector jobs, many part time, which pay poverty-level wages.  Many of these jobs are susceptible to technological displacement if pressure to increase wages grows.

There has been a basic shift in the role of human labor in productive activity in industrialized societies.  We are now in the throes of a technological revolution as sweeping as the original Industrial Revolution over three centuries ago, a revolution in microelectronics which, through drastic reductions in the cost of increasingly more complex and sophisticated control systems, is making possible rapid and widespread displacement of human labor by machines.

The catalog of ills goes on and on.  Inflation, while it may be temporarily abated (largely by throwing tens of millions of people out of work and ushering in the worst recession -- many call it a depression -- since the Great Depression of the 1930s), is still hanging in the wings and has started rising again in recent months.  As long as the world's political leaders persist in their mad course of ever-increasing and more grotesque spending on non-productive armaments, inflation will bedevil the world's economy.

This world economic crisis is causing enough pain and suffering in the relatively more robust industrialized economies.  But it is creating complete havoc in the Third World, where, in some countries, external debt exceeds more than half of export earnings.  So serious has the situation become that it has been argued that the Third World should wipe the slate clean by collectively repudiating its external debt and starting all over again.[1]

Nor does this exhaust the catalog of ills afflicting the world economy.  Longer term in character but no less serious in consequences is the inexorable depletion of non-renewable natural resources, including but hardly limited to petroleum.  And modern industry continues to use the world's biosphere as a sink, with the disposal of hazardous industrial waste now reaching such a critical stage that whole communities have had to be abandoned in North America as increasing efforts are made to dump such wastes in vulnerable Third World countries.

Why are we in such a mess?  There are many reasons, of course, but prominent among them are the economic ideas of Keynes.  As Robert Swann, builder, economist, originator of the Community Land Trust Movement in the U.S., and president of the E.F. Schumacher Society explains:

When John Maynard Keynes wrote his book, *The General The-*

---

[1]See "Redistribution without Justice," *Indian Express*, March 2, 1983.

*ory of Interest and Employment,* he became famous because the world saw his theory of financial manipulation by the government as the solution to the problem of unemployment. This is not to imply that Keynes was the only, nor the first to advocate such ideas, but to a large extent his name has become associated with them in academic and government circles. Ever since then virtually all of the economists trained in the United States and European universities have been taught the Theory. It has become the Bible of the economic establishment. It is true that there have been dissenters, including the Marxists, but these dissenters have received little attention within the halls of government "decision makers" in the Western economies.

At the risk of over-simplification Keynes' "monetary" and "fiscal" policies, which are the basis of what is often called a "managed economy," all add up to trying to stimulate the economy if it is sluggish or slow it down if it is over-stimulated. The economy is stimulated or cooled off merely by increasing or decreasing taxes (fiscal policies), or by printing money to create inflation or reducing the supply of money if inflation is getting out of hand (monetary policies). Keynes said, "a little inflation is a good thing." By this he meant that, with inflation, people are encouraged to spend more, and spending stimulates the economy. He did not, of course, explain that inflation can lead to disasters, perhaps worse disasters than unemployment. In the same way, reducing taxes is supposed to give the consumer more spendable money and therefore stimulate the economy, or vice versa.[2]

Swann goes on to explain that for a time Keynes' ideas seemed to work because of the need to do something about massive unemployment during the Great Depression, the enormous stimulus to demand that occurred with the Second World War, and changes in technology, especially communications and transportation, that made it possible to exploit the entire world's resources at an ever-increasing rate.

Today the situation has changed and it has become increasingly clear that high technology is beginning to reach a plateau of development (after all, "labor saving" can only go so far) and the limits of the world's resources have begun to loom on the horizon. Thus, we have "stagflation," with increasing unemployment and increasing inflation occurring simultaneously -- a condition which has confounded most Keynesians, although Keynes himself may have foreseen it with his famous statement *"for a time* we must pretend that fair is foul and

[2]Robert Swann, "Land, Land Trusts, and Employment," *Green Revolution* (York, Pennsylvania: School of Living, 1977), p. 17.

foul is fair." Whether he meant it this way or not, we have been de-
pleting the world's resources and polluting the environment as the
means with which to maintain the value of the dollar. His devotees
have forgotten the first part of the statement and are puzzled over
what to do now since he left no further instructions.

There is, of course, still some slack in the system for the
economists and politicians to use in postponing galloping inflation
for awhile. There is still a large portion of the population who are
not well fed, well clothed, or well housed, and direct government
subsidies -- if politically possible -- to those groups may continue for
a time to prop up the system and stave off runaway inflation. This is
only relatively true, of course; government subsidies for real needs
are not necessarily as inflationary as guns and bombs, but bureaucratic red tape can add enormous inflationary costs. But these subsidies cannot forever be advanced without a reduction in the subsidies to the big corporations in the form of defense spending. We
cannot much longer have "guns and butter" too.[3]

To the discredited Keynesian economic theory can now be added the
equally implausible underlying proposition of supply side economics --
namely, that radical tax reductions will so stimulate economic growth as
actually to boost government revenue, thereby eliminating budget deficits,
while simultaneously generating enough jobs to keep everybody employed
at decent wages. Under the Reagan Administration in the U.S., this had
become a cruel hoax for soaking the poor to benefit the rich.

In the despair and frustration generated by the failure of such
"mainstream" economic ideas lies the opportunity of revitalizing communities by rebuilding their economies, literally, from the ground up. It is
a melancholy fact of life that in order to bring about significant change,
conditions have to get bad enough for a sizable proportion of people that
they are prepared to accept, if not work themselves, for meaningful
change.

Hence, there is hope for depressed communities and people de-
prived of the opportunity for meaningful and productive work. That hope
lies in using tools for community economic transformation that place the
well being of the people and the sustainability of economic activity in the
environment at the center of their concern.

In the remaining chapters of this book are described some of these
tools and the concepts underlying them, beginning with that most fundamental resource, next to its people, of any community -- namely, land and
natural resources. This section is followed by one on techniques of and
institutions for community self-management, including worker-owned
businesses and producer-consumer cooperatives. The next section is de-

-----------------------

[3]Ibid.

voted to community banking and currency, including techniques of self-financing. While some of these tools and concepts may seem visionary, they are rooted in the practical experiences of the principal contributors to this book, and many of them have actually been tried or are now being tested in real life situations.

These ideas, techniques, and institutional arrangements reflect the work and thinking of Robert Swann, already identified above; Shann Turnbull, Australian businessman and management consultant and exponent of new arrangements for individual and community control of productive assets, social services, and credit, which he calls social capitalism; and the late George Benello, businessman, teacher, and author, who was a leading expert on worker-managed industries.

The pioneering and often disarmingly simple and straightforward ideas and approaches discussed in this book in turn have drawn upon earlier efforts at introducing new directions in economic thought and social reform. The origins of these ideas and approaches go back at least as far as Henry George's concern with trying to find ways of capturing the "unearned" increase in land values for community use.

Other sources include the late economist Ralph Borsodi's search for more socially appropriate solutions to such fundamentals as a stable international currency and determination of which economic resources should be possessed by the individual and which by the community, and Rudolph Steiner's ideas on basic economic issues articulated in such works as his series of lectures published under the title *World Economy*. Yet another source for these ideas and approaches is the ESOP (Employee Stock Ownership Plan) movement, which has been spearheaded by Louis Kelso and which, for all its defects and limitations, is the most widely practiced form of worker ownership of productive assets today in North America.

These and other sources are complemented by E.F. Schumacher's *Small is Beautiful: Economics as if People Mattered*, which nurtures what is called today the appropriate technology movement, and the works of many others. The final part of the book is consequently a bibliography which, while in no sense comprehensive, does try to reflect something of the diversity of thinking and experience on which the tools and concepts for community economic transformation presented here are based.

# Chapter 2

# ROOT CAUSES OF THE WORLD'S ECONOMIC BREAKDOWN

*Shann Turnbull*

The two basic causes of economic breakdown in countries with private property market economies today are set out in Figure 1. These are:

- The rules used for owning land and corporations;
- Government-created monopoly money systems supported by central banking.

The direct, secondary, and higher order problems created by these root causes are shown in the boxes in Figure 1. Underneath eight of these boxes, there are dotted lines indicating how problems feed back to reinforce problems which contributed to their own creation. This creates a vicious circle that accelerates the breakdown.

The monopolization of money by governments has occurred since money evolved over 6,000 years ago. Wheat and barley were widely used as money around 5000 B.C. This was both a decentralized and democratic form of money as there were many producers. The ownership of iron, copper, silver, and gold mines were generally monopolized by the local rulers of the city states or nations. As a result, agrarian monies were soon replaced by base metal monies under the control of the local rulers by 3000 B.C. This allowed them to finance their local wars by increasing

## Figure 1

## ROOT CAUSES OF ECONOMIC BREAKDOWN

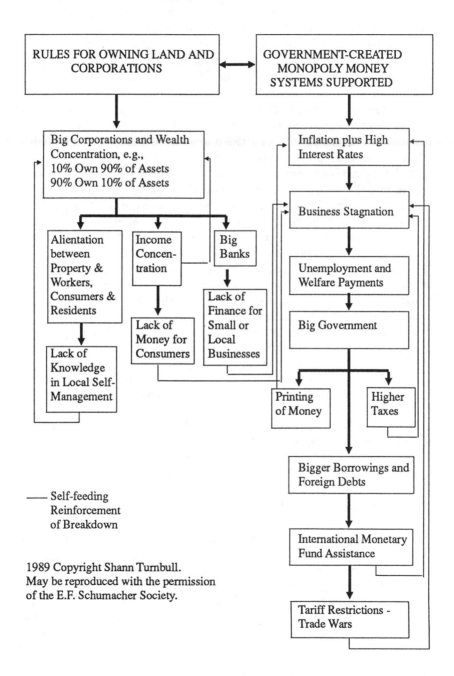

RULES FOR OWNING LAND AND CORPORATIONS ↔ GOVERNMENT-CREATED MONOPOLY MONEY SYSTEMS SUPPORTED

Big Corporations and Wealth Concentration, e.g.,
10% Own 90% of Assets
90% Own 10% of Assets

Alientation between Property & Workers, Consumers & Residents

Income Concen-tration

Big Banks

Lack of Knowledge in Local Self-Management

Lack of Money for Consumers

Lack of Finance for Small or Local Businesses

Inflation plus High Interest Rates

Business Stagnation

Unemployment and Welfare Payments

Big Government

Printing of Money

Higher Taxes

Bigger Borrowings and Foreign Debts

International Monetary Fund Assistance

Tariff Restrictions - Trade Wars

—— Self-feeding Reinforcement of Breakdown

1989 Copyright Shann Turnbull.
May be reproduced with the permission
of the E.F. Schumacher Society.

the production of base metals which had little local intrinsic value. Inflation resulted which often led to domestic unrest and the overthrow of the local ruler. History has been repeating itself ever since.

Some notable examples of government-induced inflation and economic breakdown through the monopolization of money occurred in the Roman Empire and eighteenth-century France, during the American Civil War, and in Germany in 1923. More notable but far less known were the many stable and enduring monetary systems developed in all corners of the globe. Many were based on agrarian products or artifacts. Certificates of deposit printed on parchment were used in Roman times and paper money became popular in China in the eleventh century.

It took the Chinese 500 years to learn that government-created monopoly monetary systems did not work. However, privately issued paper money convertible into a specified amount of a given commodity like a brick of tea did work. Competing private paper currencies which represented certificates of deposit for a given amount of a commodity continued in use after state paper money was abandoned in China during the sixteenth century. The same type of system existed in the United States and a number of other countries in the nineteenth century. The lesson of history is that competing private commodity-backed currencies work while government monopoly money does not.

Central banking with paper money is an innovation of the twentieth century. While this innovation has increased the stability of individual banks, it has done so at the cost of decreasing the stability of the currency, and indeed the whole financial system.

The great advantage of a decentralized system with multiple competing currencies is that any failure in one part of the system would allow the healthy parts to take over. In the past, just the threat of competitors created prudence in money management as it does today to a much lesser degree between the competing monopoly currencies of nations.

While the relative value between the monopoly currencies of nations is determined by market pressures, the lending of currencies between nations is being taken over by institutions less and less influenced by market forces. As the world's monetary problems increase, these institutions are forced to disregard market forces and adopt procedures to safeguard their own operations and those of the international monetary systems. This is producing two results:

- The monopoly currency systems of independent nations are being locked together through multilateral monetary institutions like the World Bank, International Monetary Fund, and the Bank of International Settlements;
- The institutional innovations currently being devised to avoid both defaults by borrowing countries and failure in the leading banks of the First World are producing a collective debasement of the world's strongest currencies.

Provided the unexpected does not happen and the multilateral financial institutions are sufficiently nimble in changing their operations so neither a borrowing country or a lending bank has to be declared bankrupt, then an abrupt collapse of the global financial system will be avoided. This will be achieved by various complex and esoteric institutional procedures which will largely obscure the simple fact that more money is being created to prop up the leading banks and the countries which are having difficulty paying back their loans. In short, to avoid a breakdown of the whole system, the lesser evil of a steady breakdown of the value of world currencies is being undertaken.

There is no other acceptable political alternative for the world's financial system but to inflate out of its present predicament. It is only through the inflation of the lending currencies that the value of the loans to countries which have overborrowed can be reduced. By this device, the loans will be steadily forgiven. The loss will be incurred not by the lending banks but by all the fixed interest investors and depositors using the lending currencies. It is for this reason that lenders are now seeking an interest rate substantially higher than the inflation rate.

The result of inflation and high interest rates as shown in Figure 1 is business stagnation, both increasing the cost and risk of doing business. This inhibits the start-up or expansion of new activities and forces many activities which otherwise would succeed to fail. Those that survive are less profitable while the uncertainty introduced by inflation has increased the risks.

Since well over half of the private-sector work force in many market economy countries is typically employed by small businesses and a large percentage of the small businesses typically fail during their first five years even in good times, unemployment increases rapidly with business stagnation. This increases the cost of government unemployment and other welfare benefits at a time the government is collecting less tax because corporations are making less profits, personal incomes are down, and the number of taxable individuals decreases.

Thus, the cost and size of government increases while the size and profitability of the private sector decreases. Yet, it is the private sector which must support the cost of government. This can be done directly through higher taxes or indirectly through the government borrowing or printing more money. These methods all reinforce business stagnation. Higher taxes reduce the viability of business as do printing more money, which creates more inflation, or domestic borrowings by the government, which increases interest rates. Overseas borrowings in excess can put the country into a debt trap where it must borrow even more money to repay just the interest, let alone the principal, of previous foreign loans.

Countries caught in the debt trap need to subject themselves to the economic policies prescribed by the International Monetary Fund (IMF) to enable them to obtain financial assistance and debt rescheduling. The policies imposed by the IMF are usually anti-inflationary and seek to reduce imports relative to exports. In the country seeking assistance, inflation may be restrained often with the cost of higher interest rates and so more business stagnation.

To provide such assistance on a growing scale, the IMF has had to increase the amount of funds it has at its disposal. The result, as noted above, is an expansion in the money supply of the lending nations. Thus, while IMF assistance may result in higher interest rates and lower inflation in the borrowing countries, this assistance is likely to increase inflationary pressures in the lending countries.

With or without IMF encouragement, countries caught in the debt trap are forced to restrict imports so as to preserve their earnings of foreign exchange to pay the costs of their foreign borrowings. Import quotas and higher import tariffs are common techniques to provide protection and encourage import substitution. A trade "war" is created when exporting countries start to retaliate by reducing their imports from countries that create barriers to their exports. Everyone becomes a loser as such trade restrictions decrease economic efficiency and increases costs.

Business stagnation is also encouraged by the current rules adopted in private property market economies for owning land and corporations. These is no business reason for these rules to create perpetual claims or to be static. Rules created by society can be changed by society. The current rules evolved in quite a different social and physical environment than exists today. They were developed when:

- The output of goods and services depended more upon labor hours than technology;
- The world's population was only a fraction of that today;
- Natural resources and the ability of the environment to absorb pollution was considered infinite; and
- Governments perpetuated slavery, human exploitation in general, and foreign colonization.

Indeed, it was from the imperial ambitions of the English sovereigns that corporations created by Royal Charter were provided with the rights of perpetual succession. A feature of the English Joint Stock Company Act of 1846 provided for the creation of an artificial person (corporate body) without the need for a Royal Charter. The early European concept of a corporation, such as the Société Anonomie (S.A.) established by common law practice for purely pragmatic commercial purposes, was always created for a limited time period. When European countries enshrined their common law corporate concept into their civil laws, they followed the English practice of providing for perpetual claims to resources. The concept of creating a corporate body for a limited time period, however, still exists in countries and states that were once European colonies such as Indonesia and the state of Louisiana in the U.S.

The corporate concept was created as an instrument of political colonization, rather than as a business structure, in order to pool finances and provide the contributors with limited liability. The ability of corporations to obtain claims over resources in perpetuity now creates in both multinational and domestic corporations economic inefficiencies and inequities which are difficult to identify with conventional economic analysis based on concepts of profits.

The cash flow concepts of investment analysis used by corporate executives are generally limited to a period of less than 20 years. There are many sound practical reasons for this approach. Most plants and machinery wear out during this period or their output becomes obsolescent. In any event, it is not possible to forecast competition, costs, and revenues so far ahead. Even if reliable estimates could be made, the value of receiving any cash so far in the future would fade into insignificance when that same cash at the bank today could be accumulating with compound interest and without so much uncertainty. Investment decisions are made in practice without relying on receiving any returns after a relatively short period. With today's uncertainties of political, social, and technological change that often represents a period less than 10 years.

Investment returns received after such a "time horizon" selected by the investor are a bonus representing profits in excess of the incentive required to bring forth the investment. They can be properly labeled "surplus profits." The moral and technical rationale for a market economy is that competition will limit excess or surplus profits. The emergence of surplus profits arises from corporations being creating with ownership rules which are both perpetual and static. The solution is to adopt ownership claims which are limited in time and are dynamic. The present rules for owning things through corporations are inconsistent with the moral and technical justification for a private property market economy.

Indeed, some political thinkers have been prepared to throw the baby out with the bath water by rejecting private property market economies in favor of socialism or communism. A more constructive approach is to change the rules of corporate ownership to make them moral, efficient, and equitable, and so more politically appealing.

The concept of surplus profits is one reason why less than 10 percent of individuals typically own more than 90 percent of corporate assets in market economies. Corporations provide an efficient mechanism for aggregating wealth through the capture of surplus profits which cannot be detected by traditional accounting and economic analysis. The result has been emergence of giant corporations. These corporations often own as much as 50 percent of the productive assets of a market economy but employ only 15 to 20 percent of the private-sector work force. This represents an even smaller proportion of the total work force when 25 to 30 percent of the workers of a market economy are typically employed by the public sector. The productive success of giant corporations is dependent upon their federating many small operating units which often employ only around 250 people.

The operating efficiency of work groups decreases as their size increases. The economies of large-scale production arise from the technology used, not the number of workers. This is a fundamental distinction frequently overlooked in economic analysis. For example, in 1982 the Japanese only required 85 labor hours to make an automobile, while U.S. manufacturers required over 76 percent more labor hours. Giant corporations obtain a competitive advantage from the value of the technology they use. This in turn provides another competitive advantage over small enterprises as the cost in man hours to organize a $100,000,000 financing may be little different from organizing $1,000,000. This is as true for the source of finance as it is for the borrower. Giant corporations beget big banks and big banks beget giant corporations.

The economies of scale in financial institutions can likewise be quite dramatic. This not only applies to the operating costs of the institution but in its ability to attract and lend funds. As a result, it is difficult for small institutions to survive unless there are non-economic reasons to provide support such as may be found in credit unions. The costs of approving one loan of $10 million may be no different from one of $1,000,000, or even $100,000. As a result, it is not in the self-interest of big banks to service small businesses. Small businesses are likely to represent a higher risk for the banks for all of the reasons described above.

With the monopoly currency system this can strangle new enterprise. Small business is the seedbed for innovation and increased productivity. Studies have shown that far more innovations are created by small entrepreneurs than big corporate research departments. With private competing currencies, as much credit can be created on a decentralized local basis as there are profitable business opportunities. Credit cannot be rationed and allocated to the big corporations when a monopoly currency system is not in place. Monopoly currencies increase the competitive advantage of both big banks and big business over small locally owned and controlled enterprises. This advantage is reinforced by the current rules for owning corporate assets.

The current rules for owing land, like those for owning corporations, also create another subtle mechanism to generate bonus economic values. In land, these bonus economic values are called windfall gains or unearned increments in value. They are called unearned because they increments in land value are not created by the landowner either directly or indirectly through any of his employees, lessees, or users of the land. The windfall gains are created by activities of his neighbors and by local and higher government authorities, making the region in which the land is owned more desirable or productive.

These activities are referred to by economists as "externalities." The conversion of rural land to urban provides an example. The increase in land value created by the conversion is not created by the owner in any way. It is entirely due to external investment in roads, pavements, water, sewage, power, communications, schools, hospitals, shopping centers, and other services. The result is that the landowner accumulates greater economic value from public expenditures and expenditures made by his neighbors and local commercial interests.

While land taxes may recover some of the public costs over many years, these costs are not incurred by the short-term owner or speculator. The inequities are compounded when the owner leases his land to others to use. The non-owners are then put in the position of making the owner richer.

Different rules are required for owning land and corporations which provide the necessary incentive for bringing forth new enterprise and investments, but which distribute values in excess of that incentive to those who contribute most to these values. With a corporation, this would mean the employees, customers, and other "stakeholders" who make a contribution to its viability. With land, neighbors and tenants need to be included in the ownership and control arrangements according to the contribution they make to windfall gains.

These arrangements would reduce the alienation which is currently widespread between stockholders and employees, managers and consumers, landowners and tenants. They would enhance and restore political legitimacy to private property market economies. They would also increase economy efficiency for a number of reasons that are explained when alternative arrangements for owning land and corporations and for managing productive assets and activities are described elsewhere in this book. It is only through such arrangements that the root causes in the breakdown of the world's political economy can be overcome.

# COMMUNITY STEWARDSHIP OF LAND AND NATURAL RESOURCES

# Chapter 3

# ALTERNATIVES TO OWNERSHIP: LAND TRUSTS AS LAND REFORM

*Robert Swann*

In those countries where traditional land reform (redistribution of land to private owners as initiated by the central state -- examples include Japan, Taiwan, Iran, some South American countries) has taken place, redistribution of land has resulted in some cases (Taiwan, for instance) in higher production and improved social and political conditions. In other cases, however, loss of production, and over a period of time, recycling of land ownership back to a handful of owners has taken place. One reason for this result (where only land is redistributed by government order) is a breakdown in the local credit systems (usually controlled by the former large landowners) and market systems.

In India, Israel, and Tanzania, however, a different approach has been taken which, while encouraged by the state, remains a private land reform movement. In each of these countries, although differing in some respects, the concept of individual or state ownership of land has been replaced by community ownership and control. In these cases, land is leased by the community to individuals or families but equity in ownership of homes or other improvements is retained by the individual or family. In this way, private initiative has been encouraged and productivity (and morale) has remained high, but reversion of ownership to a few land owners is permanently prevented. Since these land reform movements have been voluntary and private, they have not engendered the resentment and resistance, with its resulting dislocations, which have been counterproductive in other countries.

In the U.S., a variation on this community approach to land reform referred to as the Community Land Trust has been gaining momentum in the face of public apathy over land reform in general. Both the Community Land Trust (CLT) movement and the environmental movement have in common the notion of trusteeship or stewardship of land rather than the traditional concept of ownership. However, while the "land trust" movement of the environmentalists is aimed at protection of the land only, the CLT movement is aimed at increasing the productivity of the land by reducing speculation and providing access to land by individuals and families who otherwise lack such access. CLTs operate in both urban and rural areas and today a certain convergence is taking place between CLTs and conservation land trusts.

In the lower Berkshire County in Massachusetts, farming has for many years been superseded in the economy by the pressure for summer homes and housing coming from the metropolitan corridor (from Boston to New York). At the same time forestry, which has considerable potential in the region prevails in general throughout New England, but the region has become heavily (85 percent) dependent upon sources of food from the outside (California, Texas, Florida). This vulnerability to increasingly high costs of food as well as the threat of possible sudden loss of food supply (truckers' strikes, gasoline shortages, etc.) has created a strong social and political movement which is attempting to deal with this problem through legislative action (reduced property taxes for farmers, purchase development rights, and so forth). In part, at least, because the programs are expensive and must be paid for from taxes levied on the urban population, they have been only peripherally effective and probably will remain so. Another major reason for their ineffectiveness is that they do not involve local people in significant ways, a characteristic failure in traditional land reform as well. Other factors in the failure of traditional land reform (loss of credit infrastructure, reversion of land to a few landowners who control credit structures, a failure of market development, etc.) are met more or less successfully by CLTs.

An important aspect of the CLT approach to land use and long-range tenure change is to utilize existing laws (such as conservation easements) to encourage land use management for long-range agriculture and forest management. An example of this is the Forest Land Trust, which the CLT in the Southern Berkshires is sponsoring for the region. Under this program, the CLT promotes land pooling under a single management plan of varied tracts of forest land held by up to 35 landowners. Incentives to landowners (aside from wildlife and forest conservation) include both income, property tax, and estate tax advantages as well as increased income from professional forestry management. Advantages to the CLT and the region in general include increased income for management (to the CLT) and increased employment and long-range stability (to the community). The program, which does not require sale of fee simple title on the part of landowners, brings the CLT into contact with the larger landowners in the region. This provides an opportunity for education regarding land that may result in future purchase, gift, or partial gift of land to the CLT for its long-range leasing program. (Forest Land Trusts are further described in Chapter 5.)

Failure to provide credit has often been the cause of the floundering of traditional land reform movements. The Community Land Trust in the Southern Berkshires is acting as a catalyst to initiate an investment program that can benefit not only the CLT in particular but many small (or large) enterprises (both for profit and non-profit) in the entire region itself. Referred to as the Self-Help Association for a Regional Economy (SHARE), this program is being administered by an existing local bank. Funds for local use are being solicited from the entire local population, but a separate board has been set up to establish criteria for making loans and investments and to monitor them. These criteria place the emphasis for making loans or investment on the degree to which such loans impact favorably on local employment, regional self-sufficiency and the environment, and will include, of course, mortgages on CLT land and related enterprises (such as food processing, forest management, etc.) as priorities, as well as on cooperative ownership of industry to ensure better distribution of income.

# Chapter 4

# THE COMMUNITY IMPACT OF LAND TRUSTS

*Robert Swann*

Land trusts can have an extraordinary "ripple effect" on the economy and ecology of an entire community. Below is a hypothetical example of what could happen in any Northeastern community in the U.S. if all of the land in the community were held in trust.

In the first place, let us say that the entire area might consist of 20,000 acres (about average for a Massachusetts town). In this area, we would have perhaps 70-80 percent forested land and the rest open space devoted to farming or built up in housing, industry, etc. (such a distribution is typical in New England). Presently (before going into trust) the forested land is not being used for lumber except to a limited degree -- and only a small portion is used for firewood -- or sometimes for pulpwood for paper production. In general, such forest land is totally underutilized because of the former pattern of ownership, which generally consists of small parcels (20-300 acres), none of them large enough to justify sustained-yield forest management. Moreover, the former owners tended to view the land as an investment, to be held for future sale at, hopefully, a good capital gain or high speculative price. Holding the land for a high speculative price has eliminated the possibility of anyone buying it for forest management purposes because it would be too expensive at the "speculation price" per acre for such purposes -- in fact, it would also be too expensive for farming. Thus, the farmers who became too old to farm have usually sold their farms off to non-farmers, either speculators or people rich enough to be able to afford to buy their "piece of the country" without farming. Even when the land was used, the economic rent went into private hands and did not tend to accrue to the benefit of the community, thus minimizing the impact on local employment.

But now it is held in trust (never mind how it got there -- we will discuss that later). Now it can be put into sustained-yield management, because the forest area is large enough (15,000-16,000 acres) for good management, and no longer is being held for speculation. What does this mean in terms of employment? In the first place, it means that for every 300-400 acres the project can employ one person full time to clean out and thin out the trees (dead wood, poor species, etc.) so that the remaining trees selected for lumber will grow more rapidly. This employs about 50 or so persons who probably were not formerly employed within the community. We will also need four to six full-time foresters to manage the forests. Secondly, the weed trees which are cleaned out will go into one or more of the following markets: energy (firewood or wood chips), pulpwood (paper), or the newly developing cattle food market.[1] Since these markets will in turn stimulate new local industries, more new jobs will be created. In addition, over time, good lumber will be grown in these forests which will bring a higher price, require logging operations, and provide increased employment, as well as put new, better quality lumber into the local market for housing and wood industries.

At the same time, since the farmland has been freed of speculative demands, it too can go back into production and once again provide employment for young people anxious to get back into farming but frustrated at all points because of the high cost of land. With increased production from forests and farmland, local taxes assessed through the trust as the price of leasing the land will mean that the town can provide better services, better roads, better schools, etc. without burdening the older home-owning taxpayers. These services will also increase employment and improve everybody's standard of living. New housing for the new employees in the forest and farm industries will also bring increased employment, but because of the trust, this housing can be planned to go on the most suitable land from an ecological and planning viewpoint -- not simply where land can be purchased -- thus saving extra costs of unplanned development. Moreover, since the land is not purchased, the cost of the housing can be lower in cost with local employees receiving first option on purchase.

Finally, then, how is this to come about? Because the people in the

---

[1]In those parts of the country where forest land is not available, other sources of "bio-mass" (e.g., rapid-growing crops) could substitute for wood as an energy source, providing the land is available at reasonable cost.

town decide for themselves that they will set up the trust and voluntarily give the land to the trust. After all, they will be the major beneficiaries when increased employment means that their sons and daughters can find employment near home and the entire town becomes revitalized. But if not enough of them are attracted to this proposition, then there would be other direct financial benefits derived from increased productivity of forests and farmland. These would go directly to the former landowners and indirectly, through improved services and increased local business, to all residents.[2]

One other important point which Rudolf Steiner makes in his *World Economy* is that not only have we "decommoditized" the land (by taking it out of the speculative market) but we have also "decapitalized" the land. That is, no longer is it necessary to draw on the capital markets (including local banks) to buy the land. Thus, the capital formerly tied up in land is free to be used for other kinds of investment. These may be mortgages on housing, new industries such as solar energy, farm improvements, etc., or they may go into "spiritual" needs such as new kinds of education, or "spiritual work," which, as Steiner points out, are really the most economically productive for the future.

There will be those who will sneer at the above as a mere "idealistic" dream. It may be so, but it has never been tried. No such vision has ever been put before a community, large or small, where the community (it would require less than a majority to put it into practice) could make the decision. In any case, it needs to be tested. As inflation and unemployment grow, I suspect that many communities will be ready to try new approaches, particularly when they realize that none of the government programs are working except in peripheral ways.

---

[2]Even if the cost of such an undertaking were subsidized by the federal government, the funds thus expended would "leverage" far more employment than any other kind of subsidy. Economists have calculated that for every family which moves into an urban area from a rural area, about $50,000-60,000 in local municipal or federal subsidies are required in order to cover the increased load on public services (fire, police, road repair and maintenance, etc.), health and welfare, job training, and so forth. Only a fraction of this amount would be required in rural areas -- if land were made available -- to accomplish the same purposes.

# Chapter 5

# DIFFERENT TYPES
# OF LAND TRUSTS

The label "land trust" has been affixed to organizations with purposes ranging from rehabilitating burned-out tenements to marking and maintaining a system of bridle and foot paths. Although the various types of land trusts are linked by a common thread (i.e., ownership and management of resources by a private organization in trust for the public good), it will be less confusing in the long run to separate the various land trusts into three easily definable and distinguishable categories.

**Land Conservation Trusts** (LCTs) are land trusts whose main purpose is to protect and preserve natural areas. In addition, LCTs often engage in environmental education programs, sponsor various outdoor recreation events, and serve as local watchdogs with regard to issues related to conservation of natural resources.

**Community Land Trusts** (CLTs), on the other hand, do not have the preservation of natural areas as their major objective. They are chiefly motivated by egalitarian concerns, such as providing farmland, community gardens, and low-cost housing to members of the public who would ordinarily be denied access to them.

Another application of the CLT concept is the **Forest Land Trust** (FLT) whose objective is to bring unmanaged forestland into timber production. This is done by first having a group of landowners convey their development rights to the FLT; then the landowners form a partnership and pool their timber resources in a long-range forestry program managed by the partnership and/or the FLT. Such a plan would increase the value of the timber severalfold, provide additional income to the landowners, and furnish them with significant reductions in their income, estate, and property taxes.

Each of these types of land trusts is described separately in Chapters 7, 8, and 12. Additional details of Community Land Trusts are given in Chapters 9, 10, and 11, while Chapter 6 compares CLTs and Land Conservation Trusts.

# Chapter 6

# COMPARISON OF COMMUNITY LAND TRUSTS AND LAND CONSERVATION TRUSTS

CLTs are similar to traditional Land Conservation Trusts (LCTs) in that both are dedicated to land stewardship and protection of the land from profit-oriented exploitation and are intended to be sensitive to environmental issues. They differ in that CLTs do not seek or are often unable to obtain tax-exempt status, their land is generally not legally bound to remain undeveloped in perpetuity, and, as noted above, CLTs emphasize productive use of land, in contrast to the LCTs' usual proclivity toward preservation of natural areas.

Notwithstanding these differences, a commonality of purpose exists between CLTs and LCTs that would make a collaboration of their efforts desirable in several instances. For example, if a LCT acquired a large parcel of farmland and desired to keep it in production, then it could lease or convey the property to a CLT, which would maintain the parcel as a working farm.

The above example makes sense for at least two reasons. First, since one of the major purposes of Land Conservation Trusts is to preserve the beauty and rural character of the community, they have an interest in seeing that working farms, an attractive but ever-diminishing element of the landscape in the Northeast and some other regions of the country, remain in operation. Second, the active members of a LCT usually do not have the time, the expertise, or even the desire to do the farming themselves and would be glad to have a CLT run the operation.

# Chapter 7

# LAND CONSERVATION TRUSTS

Land Conservation Trusts (LCTs) are private, non-profit conservation organizations that seek to acquire land for the protection of natural areas. They can exist in either of two legal forms: corporation or charitable trust. Little difference exists between these structures, and the decision to proceed with a corporate or trust format usually hinges on the preference of the attorney enlisted to help draft the organizational document.

The only significant difference between the corporate or charitable trust format is that charitable corporations are primarily regulated by statute (Chapter 180 of the Massachusetts General Laws, by way of example; comparable statutes in other states), while the charitable trusts remain largely governed by the common law (i.e., the traditional laws which the United States inherited from England and which are expressed in judicial opinions). This means that a lawyer drafting a declaration of trust may be more on his own than if he had chosen to incorporate, as incorporation forms are readily available and their contents spelled out by statute.

It is important for both legal forms of organizations that the documents empower the organization to do everything that it may want to do in pursuit of its charitable objectives as well as provide for amendment of the documents in the case of any unforeseen events. For example, if a parcel of land donated to a land conservation trust, and originally of significant conservation value, later loses that value because of development on the abutting land, and if no provision exists in the organization's by-laws, articles of incorporation, or declaration of trust for the sale of the land for purposes other than conservation, the LCT would have to go through a lengthy court proceeding in order to become legally entitled to sell the land.

Private organizations like Land Conservation Trusts play an important role in the protection of natural areas and open spaces. LCTs can solicit and receive private donations of conservation land and many LCTs have acquired most, if not all, of their land holdings through donations. LCTs will often accept parcels of land that for various reasons (e.g., the parcel is too small, odd-shaped, inaccessible, or the donor's deed restrictions are too cumbersome) are unacceptable to public bodies. LCTs can act quickly to secure vital pieces of conservation land that have suddenly come onto the market, since these organizations are not as encumbered by red tape as are public bodies, such as town conservation commissions, in most situations.

Although conservation commissions and other town boards are legally entitled to acquire land outside municipal boundaries as long as the land is used for a municipal purpose, they may face substantial political obstacles in acquiring important conservation land outside a town. A Land Conservation Trust in this situation could solve the problem by securing the parcel.

Land Conservation Trusts are particularly adept at raising money for the acquisition of conservation land, especially for large and/or critical natural areas, even if the money or the land is eventually transferred to the town. This is of prime importance when the funds appropriated to the conservation commission for their land acquisition program have run dry before all the lands designated for protection have been purchased.

Land Conservation Trusts can be effective publicity agents, providing a vehicle for the public expression of conservation values outside the sticky realm of local politics. LCTs can also prod slow-moving conservation commissions into action. (The reverse has also been known to happen.)

The fact that Land Conservation Trusts can and do play a vital role in the protection of natural areas should not draw attention from the outstanding records of some conservation commissions. Many communities have such active conservation commissions that the need for a local Land Conservation Trust is largely obviated.

Why not rely on national or state land conservation trusts such as the Nature Conservancy to undertake all the private action necessary for natural areas and open space preservation? Local LCTs are not in competition with groups like the Nature Conservancy; rather, LCTs supplement the efforts of the latter groups by giving donors the option of keeping their gift in local hands. Many landowners are sentimental about their home towns and would like to see land donations managed by a local board of trustees. In addition, national organizations may insist on an endowment to subsidize the expenses of a field staff, while a local LCT can more easily recruit abutting landowners to serve as volunteer wardens of the trust's land. No national or state organization has the ability or the desire to acquire every piece of land that has been determined to be deserving of protection. The assistance of capable local organizations is essential.

# Chapter 8

# COMMUNITY LAND
# TRUSTS

The Community Land Trust (CLT), a new approach to land tenure, is an alternative to existing landholding practices and is based on ethical distribution and rational use of resources. It is designed to hold natural resources like the land, which was created without human intervention, in trust by and for the community.

One of the CLTs most significant philosophical departures from the principles of traditional Land Conservation Trusts is the notion that the land should not be locked up, with use denied to those who could or would like to husband its natural resources and utilize its development potential in a manner consistent with conservation of natural resources.

The principal objective of most CLTs is to settle the land and put it to sensible and productive use. This is accomplished by the organization's acquiring land, retaining permanent ownership, and then providing public access to it through long-term leases with terms that protect the natural resources while allowing for productive uses of the land.

*Urban* Community Land Trusts deal primarily with improving the quality of life within city neighborhoods by using the land they acquire for community gardens, open spaces, and low-cost housing. They also serve as suitable neighborhood recipients of funding from private foundations and governmental entities.

*Rural* Community Land Trusts seek to put their acquired land into productive use by providing access to farmland for young families anad disadvantaged groups who would otherwise be priced out of the market.

# Chapter 9

# UNDERLYING CONCEPTS AND PRINCIPLES

The underlying concept of the Community Land Trust is simply the distinction made between ownership of land, which remains in the hands of the Trust for the common good, and the use of the land, which is privately held, can be transferred, and is inheritable.

The distinction between ownership and use is not itself new or radical -- much of the commercial land in London and New York City is leased by the actual users under long-term (usually 99 years) leases. What is different about the Community Land Trust is that the ownership, and therefore the power to determine ultimately how the land is used, is vested, through the Trust, in the community as a whole.

This has an important economic implication, because it enables the community to capture much of the "unearned" increase in land value for the common good while the value of improvements made on the land (such as buildings) remain to benefit the individuals who built or have bought them. In doing so, the Community Land Trust can assure that a portion of any tract of land being developed is retained for productive purposes, whether forestry or farming, and the use of that land for these purposes can be sharply reduced in cost, since that portion would not be available for private development and therefore not able to command the price of prime land for residential building sites.

The Community Land Trust also observes the principle of self-financing. While land may be acquired in other ways through gift or bequest, it can also be acquired through direct purchase at local market value.  The users of the land pay a rental to the Land Trust, which in turn uses that income to pay a conventional mortgage for the purchase of the land.

# Chapter 10

# STRUCTURE AND
# METHOD OF
# OPERATION

Most Community Land Trusts are structured as non-profit corporations without tax-exempt status. There are some Community Land Trusts that have limited themselves to serving strictly low-income persons, and these have received tax-exempt status based on that purpose. But generally the purposes of CLTs are broadly economic and although they do "subsidize" farmland, and therefore the farmer, through housing and commercial property wisely and ecologically planned, the main purpose is not strictly conservation nor strictly to aid low-income or disadvantaged persons. Rather it is a concern with fair access to and productive use of land within ecological conditions and includes the conservation-minded as well as the development-minded.

The method used by the Community Land Trust is to purchase land, then lease the rights to use it based on a land use plan for the piece as a whole. This might include use as house lots, commercial property, farming, or forestry. The commercial use would obviously have the highest use fee, the house lots next, then farming and forestry set at a low lease fee varying with actual soil conditions, topography, etc. The lease is usually written for 99 years and is automatically renewable if the terms of the lease are kept. In this way, housing pays for the major cost of land in the rural areas. Any portion of a piece of land strictly suitable for conservation purposes is given to a Land Conservation Trust. A LCT may also hold the conservation restriction on the farmland portion or forested portion, but the fee simple title stays with the Community Land Trust.

Buildings and other improvements (for instance, the establishment of an orchard) are owned by the leasee with a registered Community Land Trust and can be sold at a price established by formula with the Community Land Trust (basically cost of construction adjusted for inflation and depreciation). But the land itself cannot be sold. The lease is transferable, therefore establishing the same terms of use with the new owner of improvements. This leasing arrangement thus discourages tying up productive land for speculative purposes. House lots must be used as house lots and orchards used as orchards, not left idle and held against future needs and speculations. In this manner, the real needs in the region for productive use and not just individual interests are served. Original land use plans are designed, taking into consideration economic as well as ecological factors in the whole region.

As an example, the CLT in the Southern Berkshires has established a $50 per month lease fee per house lot on its ten-acre parcel. Such a fee is charged whether or not a parcel of land was purchased or given to the Community Land Trust. It is what was assessed as fair in the area for the intense use of land demanded by housing. Provision is made, when economically possible, to reduce that fee for elderly or low-income persons, but basically, the $50 per month fee stands. The fee is equivalent to about a $6,000 mortgage while actual land price in the area (when large amounts are bought) ranges from $2,000 to $3,000 per acre or more. Thus, every house is financing about one-and-a-half to two acres of farmland through the lease.

Community Land Trusts therefore have an advantage in that they are not dependent on government funding or the eccentricities of donors to protect farmland. A CLT has a steady source of income from leases or anticipated leases so that it can purchase or mortgage a piece of prime farmland when it comes on the market. The lease arrangement has another advantage: it ensures that farmland is used as productive farmland, not just kept as an open space backdrop to a wealthy development (a problem with the state's current program for purchase of development rights). The land use plan for a particular farm purchased by a Community Land Trust could include an orchard area or truck farming area, depending on the needs of the community. A farmer would not lease that piece unless it was his intention to work an orchard or vegetable farm. But those who would like to take on such farming would then have the opportunity without the huge capital outlay for land. This is an affirmative step toward encouraging food self-reliance in the region. In addition, any improvements that the farmer makes in terms of soil quality, new trees, or irrigation systems remain the equity of that farmer and are saleable if the farmer decides to retire from farming or move. Again, the lease arrangements with ownership of improvements take an affirmative step in encouraging soil improvements -- a major concern of environmentalists which is discouraged in some of the short-term lease arrangements that are used currently by Land Conservation Trusts.

As the farmer reaches retirement age, the same mechanisms of leased land and ownership of improvements allow for the smooth transfer of the farming aspects to a young farmer who can buy the improvements and take over the lease, leaving the older farmer still able to stay in his home but with some income for retirement.

There are tax and legal problems associated with the Community Land Trust form. Gifts of land, which when offered would give the donor a tax advantage in exchange for his donation, are not possible under the Community Land Trust agreement. Secondly, the IRS currently considers the lease fees as income to the Community Land Trust; these lease fees are therefore taxed as corporate income, reducing the kitty for purchase of additional farmland.

One way to solve these problems would be to establish two corporations. The first would act as a familiar Land Conservation Trust, receiving gifts of land, accepting conservation restrictions, and purchasing new pieces of land, and would be organized as a 501(c)(3) tax-exempt organization. The other would be a 501(c)(2) title holding company for the tax-exempt LCT. The title-holding company (possibly the Community Land Trust) would hold the fee simple title to the productive land (housing and commercial or farming and forestry, once the development rights have been removed). All income from the lease fees to the title-holding company would go back to the Land Conservation Trust. The LCT could then purchase new land, which it would turn over to the title-holding company. In such a way, donations could come through the tax-exempt LCT, but the income from the leases to the title-holding company would not be judged as taxable.

# Chapter 11

# SOME EXAMPLES OF COMMUNITY LAND TRUSTS

*Robert Swann*

The Community Land Trust in the Southern Berkshires, located in South Egremont, Massachusetts, hopes to demonstrate how dual environmental and social objectives can be realized on a specific tract of land. While paying a fair market price for the land, the Community Land Trust's plans call for ultimate densities of approximately five acres of land per household on the entire 100-acre tract it intends to purchase (currently only 10 acres are owned by the Community Land Trust). Within the limitations of current zoning regulations, it intends to site these houses in such a way as to intrude minimally on the best farm and forest land.

Similar kinds of planning where farmland and housing form an integrated pattern are being tried in different parts of the country. Some of these efforts are organized as CLTs. One such mixed planned development is in Greene County, Virginia, on a tract of 300 acres called the Farm Colony. One hundred and fifty acres are being retained as farmland for growing crops and raising cattle, while a 40-acre segment is a wooded preserve. Forty-eight homesites will occupy the remainder of the land with an overall density of about six acres per homesite.

Near Uniontown, Pennsylvania there is another example known as the New Village project sponsored by the Institute for Man and Science in

Rensselaerville, New York. This project calls for all housing to be located on 78 acres, leaving another 100 acres completely intact for open space and farming. In addition, the plan "takes advantage of natural terrain to provide solar access to each lot and to use natural drainage paths for water."

Yet another example of type of rural planning is a project proposed for a 300-acre site in Frankford Township, New Jersey, a rolling area of farms and forest. If a standard subdivision layout were used, each of the houses would be placed on a three-acre lot, making agricultural use impossible and giving the land an intensely developed look.

But according to the proposal, all of the residential units would be constructed in clusters of four to eight houses utilizing only about one-half of the total acreage and leaving the other half to be leased to farmers, subject to a deed restriction prohibiting development. Other wooded portions of the site would be open to residents for common recreational use.

In the above examples, as in the case of the CLT in the Southern Berkshires, the cost of the land itself would be primarily carried by the house lots. In this way, the remainder of the land can be offered to farmers -- at a price which they can afford to pay.

# Chapter 12

# FOREST LAND TRUSTS

### *Robert Swann*

The Forest Land Trust is a method of managing combined parcels of forest land, thereby increasing their potential as a renewable resource. The Forest Land Trust has significant financial advantages for landowners and the community and enhances the aesthetic and ecological conditions of the land.

Up to the present, several factors have discouraged management of privately held forest land, resulting in only a small percentage of privately owned forest land being managed. These factors include:

- *Size of holdings:* Most holdings are too small for landowners to afford professional forest management. (A single professional forester can manage 5,000 to 10,000 acres intensively.)
- *Short term of holdings:* The average turnover in private land in the U.S. is five to ten years. This is too short for long-term efficient forest management.
- *High cost of management and low return:* During the early years of forest management, the cost is high relative to the return.

The Forest Land Trust offers the following private benefits to counteract these factors:

- *Management plan:* The Forest Land Trust combines several

tracts of land, not necessarily contiguous, under a single management plan. Each Trust would have 2,000 to 10,000 acres in total, making it possible to obtain the economy of scale necessary for efficient management and maximum returns. Forest landowners could participate without giving up rights of ownership.

- *Permanent trust:* By placing conservation restrictions on the forested part of his/her property, the landowner ensures that the Trust will be able to develop long-term, ecologically sound management.
- *Income tax savings:* The Forest Land Trust offers landowners significant income tax savings in the very first year and for several years thereafter. These savings come about in several ways:

    By making a donation of a conservation restriction of the forested land to a qualified tax deductible organization, landowners may receive a tax deduction for the value of the restriction. The donation may be spread out over a five-year period rather than taken in the first year. The value of such a deduction is generally 50 percent of the market value but can be much higher.

    Under the Forest Land Trust plan, landowners become partners in a limited partnership for forest management. As partners they can benefit from tax deduction for the depreciation of the original capital investment and expenses in setting up the forest management operation.

    Averaging of income from the entire pool of forest land means a steady yearly income rather than harvests of one year out of ten with resulting high tax in that year.

- *Property tax savings:* The conservation restriction on land permits the landowner to request a reduction of property tax. This is comparable to property tax deductions under Act 61 in the state of Massachusetts and similar laws in other states.
- *Timber revenue insured:* Professional management can increase the value of a landowner's forest by several times through careful selective thinning and by knowledgeable marketing of timber.

It also offers the following local community benefits:

- *Ecology:* Good forest management and selective cutting opens up the forest to permit greater penetration of sunlight, which both enhances the growth of good timber trees as well as that of low-growing bushes and shrubs on which wildlife feed. Such well-managed forests, as can be seen in Europe but only rarely in the United States, are a beauty to behold and add value to the entire community.
- *Energy and employment:* Initial high cost of selective thinning is

offset through selling wood waste as fuel wood. Dead trees and tree tops from harvesting trees can be sold as wood chips by knowledgeable foresters to the waste wood energy market. A dependable supply of waste wood for energy and quality lumber can encourage other wood-related industries and provide jobs for the community.

At least two methods could be utilized in forming a Forest Land Trust. One of these is to establish a corporation (non-profit or for profit) owned by all the landowners who want to be involved in a given region. The region should not be larger than one which a forester can handle from his home within reasonable driving distance. The tracts of forest land, however, do not need to be contiguous nor equal in size. Perhaps a limit of 20 to 30 landowners would be the best number, with a total of 5,000 to 10,000 acres (or whatever is reasonable for a forester to manage). If more landowners want to be involved, a second Forest Land Trust could be established and so on.

Under Securities and Exchange Commission (SEC) law, up to 35 shareholders are permitted in a corporation (or a limited partnership) without registration. Beyond that number the corporation (or limited partnership) is required to register, the cost of which could be as high as $50,000.

Under this method, the corporation would lease the forest land on a long-term basis from each forest landowner. The lease fee paid to the landowners would be equal to the income of the corporation so that the corporation would not show a profit.

A second method would be to establish a limited partnership, in which the limited partners would be the landowners and their share of the partnership equal to the value of the forests (not the land). Under this method, a general partner could be a local management arm of the partnership and receive a fee for its management.

Each landowner will not only have a different number of acres in the pool, but also a different value applied to different acres within his/her total acreage. But a total dollar value will be established for his/her input into the corporation or limited partnership and he/she will receive a proportionate percentage of the total shares in the company, as in any stock company. Thus, if total outstanding shares equal $500,000 and one landowner holds $100,000 of value as determined by the forester(s), he/she holds 20 percent of the total outstanding stock and will receive 20 percent of net income.

Perhaps most important is the fact that because of the larger scale operations and because of intensive management, several aspects of forestry practice can be optimized. These include:

- Use of selective thinning by-products (that is, development of a market for the so-called "junk" trees).

- Better marketing as a whole.
- Consistent upgrading of the quality of the forest stands.

In order to maximize the energy potential from waste wood and all wastes in the area, including sawdust and shavings from local mills, it will be necessary to connect this waste through the use of new technology. Here is where a pyrolytic converter might be utilized to turn waste wood into energy in the form of methane, charcoal, or electricity. The major advantage of the pyrolytic converter is its efficiency (about 85 percent as opposed to a wood stove at between 40 to 60 percent) in energy conversion. Thus, by converting the methane and charcoal to electricity at competitive rates, a market for waste wood products is immediately available. A separate company or corporation might be set up to produce electricity from waste wood. Or the same corporation, or limited partnership, which composes the Forest Land Trust could be utilized in developing an energy-producing company.

A relatively new legal concept is now being used widely by conservation organizations and states which can -- and do in some cases -- purchase "development rights" (like mineral rights, water rights, or other rights) from farmers as a means of protecting farmland. Development rights can be separated from the "bundle of rights" which lawyers refer to as composing the fee simple title. The value of the development rights on land is determined by subtracting the use value from the market value. Thus, if the market value, as determined by appraisers is $1,000 per acre for a given tract of land, and the use value as forest land is $200, the development right value is $800. A landowner who makes a gift of the development rights, known as a conservation easement, is then eligible to deduct from his/her income tax an amount equal to whatever his/her tax bracket permits, using the $800 as the base.

From a legal point of view, Congress has revised the IRS tax code under Section 170(h) to require that to be eligible for the deduction the conservation easement documents must provide for some public benefit, such as public access, scenic value, watershed protection, wildlife protection, and so forth.

As far as the non-profit, tax-exempt organization is concerned, once it has accepted the gift of a conservation easement, its only role is to "monitor" the land, which means being sure that nothing is done by the landowner which is contrary to the easement agreement. In the case of a Forest Land Trust, such monitoring is virtually automatic for the 501(c)(3) organization because the purpose of the Forest Land Trust is to ensure proper care of the forests. It may well be that it is the tax-exempt organization itself that sets up the Forest Land Trust, so that the monitoring and management are both "in house."

# Chapter 13

# THE COOPERATIVE LAND BANK CONCEPT*

*Robert Swann*

More comprehensive in scope than the various types of land trusts so far discussed, but also more far-reaching in its consequences, is the Co-operative Land Bank. The concept provides:

- A means by which a community organization (i.e., non-profit or for profit corporation representing the entire neighborhood section of a city with a population of 1,000 to 30,000 persons, or an entire town) can purchase all the land and property within its territory for the benefit of the entire community virtually without the need for outside financing. This is called the self-financing principle.
- A means for retaining within the community the value (as mea-

---

*Based on a concept developed by Shann Turnbull and published in *Democratising the Wealth of Nations* (Sydney, Australia: Company Directors Association of Australia, 1975). A fuller exposition of the concept is given in a paper by Shann Turnbull presented at the United Nations Habitat Forum, Vancouver, British Columbia, June 1976, "Land Leases without Landlords." This paper is available from the author (M.A.I. Services, Pty. Ltd., GPO Box 4359, Sydney, NSW 2001, Australia) for the cost of photocopying and postage.

sured in money) created by the community through its efforts at collective and individual development, and a means of distributing or transferring this value to both the individual members of the community and to the community as a whole on a more equitable basis. In this sense, the CLB is a substitute, on a local level (and without the bureaucracy), for efforts by national governments to transfer wealth through tax and welfare systems.

The CLB accomplishes this through establishing a duplex system of land and property tenure so that the value of community land and improvements is separated from the value of private property situated within the precincts of the CLB. The value of all land and public improvements are captured by all residents becoming common stockholders, and the value of all private improvements are captured by a system of space leases over such property. The terms on which common stock are issued to residents and redeemed by the CLB provide the means to distribute the benefits and costs of community development over time and among residents on a socially desirable basis.

For example, under the present system of single land tenure, owners can increase their rents or sale price of their properties when taxpayers' money is used to make the neighborhood a more attractive place to live, from the building of new schools and hospitals to the provision of services and facilities. As a result, landowners obtain capital gains from taxpayers' money. The non-owners (renters) increase competition among themselves to rent or buy property in the area with the better services and facilities and bid up the prices received by the owners. Landlords get richer at the expense of non-owners and the taxpayers. This is grossly inequitable and economically inefficient.

The Land Bank Cooperative creates equity and efficiency by capturing the windfall gains in property so that they can be used to pay the costs of public facilities and services. Providing the windfall gains so captured are greater than the costs, no tax payments are required and community improvements will become liberated from dependence on government tax revenues. When this occurs, they may have a basis for requesting exemption from paying taxes. Taken to its logical conclusion, this in turn would make the community a more attractive place to live and increase property values even further.

Space leases over all dwellings exist in perpetuity, while they are limited to 50 years for all other private property. This allows any residual values in all private, commercial, and industrial property to revert to residents. The equity in all residential-space leases is automatically transferred from either private or community ownership to their occupiers at a rate of 2 percent per annum. While the occupiers may need to pay 2 percent higher rents, they can become owners over 50 years without paying a deposit or becoming immediately responsible for financing the cost of the associated land site, community services, and facilities. Residents who purchase and occupy residential-space leases maintain their equity and therefore all capital gains in their home. The cost of home ownership could be reduced by the cost of the associated land for pioneer home buyers in newly developed or redeveloped areas. Any surplus capital gains created by such development would still accrue to such owners through a free issue being made to them of the common stock associated with their land. The maximum number of stock units which could be held by every resident would be determined on an identical basis of, say, one unit for every square foot of land occupied.

## Features of the Cooperative Land Bank

The Cooperative Land Bank concept attracts land and property owners to place their property in the corporation (in return for stock shares) entirely on a voluntary basis because of the financial and personal advantages of doing so. Some of these financial attractions are the result of tax advantages. Shareholders of the corporation would be free of property taxes because the corporation would pay property taxes out of accrued land value increases. In addition, it could eventually assume all other forms of taxes payable to a higher echelon of government. If the CLB represents a neighborhood or a significant section of a larger taxing entity such as a municipality, it should have the necessary political strength to remove tax assessments on property improvements which are themselves the greatest disincentive to building and community improvement.

All individual residents are automatically members of the community corporation if they live in buildings situated in the corporation. Residents who are renters at the time of property acquisition will receive on a yearly basis equity in the space lease which they occupy over a 50-year period. Thus, a 2 percent equity in their living space will be given to them on a yearly basis and at the end of 50 years they will be full owners. This concept is comparable to lease/purchase plans. If they should leave at the end of ten years, for example, 20 percent of the value of the space (apartment or house) will be paid to them for their equity in their space lease. Thus, residents are encouraged to both maintain and improve their private living space and remain in the community and accrue capital gains.

Whenever residents/owners leave the community, they can offer their space to the highest bidder. This bidder, however, will be required to buy the common shares held by the resident/owner from the CLB, which will reimburse the resident/owner after "discounting" a fee for the community corporation. This fee to the community is based on a formula composed of two factors: (1) length of time which the resident/owner had lived in the community (the longer in the community the lower the fee); (2) inflationary rate of national currency. In other words, resident/owners would be compensated in part at least for inflationary loss of currency. This mechanism for capturing "unearned increment" in land values is similar to the "capital gains" tax used by the state of Vermont. The vendor would also capture a share of any demand values created in the area by it becoming more attractive and better serviced.

Only individual resident/owners would be eligible for shareholding and voting membership in the non-profit corporation. Outside corporations, industries, etc. would lease land from the community corporation but would not be eligible for shareholding or voting rights.

The principle of "one person, one vote" would be maintained by the CLB regardless of the number of shares held. Actual ownership of shares, however, would be determined by the number of square feet in the space which each resident/owner occupied. Each square foot would represent one share. Thus, 1,000 square feet = 1,000 shares. Non-resident owners or investors in space leases would not have a vote in the corporation but would be offered investment shares similar to preferred stock in commercial corporations with a minimum yearly dividend plus a participation in the capital gain aspect of the corporation. In other words, they would receive two types of equity interests creating a duplex tenure system which in this case would be preferred shares with yearly dividends without voting rights and a 50-year lease over the property.

A special type of share would be offered to resident/owners in an area which is slated for new or redevelopment or where present resident/owners (such as older people) would like to transfer to a different form of housing. In such cases, the resident/owners would be given "conversion shares" which include voting rights and which would act like a purchase voucher for a new (or different) dwelling after development has taken place. In theory at least, the financial benefits to present resident/owners would be significant. After transfer of residency has taken place, these "conversion shares" would be exchanged for common shares or "resident shares" with their associated negotiable perpetual lease over the private space which contains their dwelling.

## Advantages of the CLB Approach

The CLB approach provides financial and personal incentives for all the owners in a reasonably large area (1,000 to 30,000 population) to join together and encourage community development by transferring individual ownership to the CLB. This approach does not require a great deal of outside investment but makes investment very attractive to outside investors, if they are needed.

The CLB approach provides incentives to residents (owners or renters) to remain in the community and participate in its development. Capital gains which accrue to the whole community as the result of development will be reflected in the value of each resident's share. Incentives are likewise provided to individual owners (as well as renters) to maintain and improve their property because they can benefit directly from such improvements (as well as from improvements to the community as a whole).

Since renters in the CLB-owned buildings become automatically owners, it may be assumed that CLB buildings will be better maintained and more attractive. This provides an incentive for private owners to join the CLB by accepting space leases and shares in the corporation in return for their property. In other words, they will lose out or lose money if they do not.

The CLB concept provides incentives to commercial, institutional, and non-resident owners of land and buildings to convert their property to the CLB duplex title system in exchange for investment shares (non-voting). The CLB agrees to lease back the buildings on these lands to their former owners for a period of 50 years (if desired) without charge (except for taxes and payments required on mortgages). A lease fee will be charged for land use, however. The incentives for this exchange, besides tax advantages noted already, include the fact that investment shares in the CLB will have a market value at any time after community development, and, therefore, will free up capital (make it liquid) which otherwise is tied up in land and buildings. Alternatively, such capital as remains in CLB stock will gain in capital value more rapidly than it would before the CLB development.

# Chapter 14

# COMPARISON OF COMMUNITY LAND TRUSTS AND COOPERATIVE LAND BANKS*

*Shann Turnbull,*
*Robert Swann,*
*and Others*

*This dialogue on similarities of and differences between Community Land Trusts and Cooperative Land Banks is based upon correspondence between Shann Turnbull in Australia and several other persons in North America sharing his interest in alternative approaches to land ownership and use, including Robert Swann, then with the Institute for Community Economics in Cambridge, Massachusetts.*

*Excerpted and adapted from Margaret Munro-Clark, ed., *Alternative Modes of Land Tenure: A Comparison of Two Models* (Sydney: Ian Buchan Fell Housing Research Unit, School of Architecture, University of Sydney, 1982).

## Differences between the CLB and CLT Concepts

Responding to a suggestion by Robert Swann that a common language be adopted to describe the commonalities between CLBs and CLTs, Turnbull pointed out that while they do involve similar objectives and concepts, there are also some basic differences, one of them being quite fundamental. This difference lies in the kind of equity in land and public assets conferred by owner-membership in a CLB as Turnbull envisages it.

## Negotiable Collective Equity

The most important difference between a CLB and a CLT is that the CLT has what Louis Kelso refers to as "sterilized ownership" of the common assets. That is, there is no negotiable interest in collective assets, and so no way for market forces to indicate through the pricing mechanism the value of community property. Not only is there no way to evaluate the utility value of community assets, but the economic incentive for each member of the community to maintain and improve such assets is substantially reduced.

These shortcomings do not exist in the CLB, which issues residential shares. The issue and redemption price of these shares provide a way to relate the market price of community assets to each individual according to how he may have contributed to their value.

A CLT could easily be modified to obtain the characteristics of a CLB. For example, a CLT which charged "key money" or a "joining fee" would gain thereby a feature that could function in a similar way to the residual shares of a CLB. All differences are matters of degree.

Community or collective ownership without a pricing mechanism to make explicit the value of community membership lacks the information feedback system which, in Turnbull's model, would serve to provide automatic checks and balances in the social organization of the CLB. His argument is that regulation by such self-correcting means is a superior alternative to using the explicit information that would be afforded by a bureaucratic "command system," because the former operates more openly and more democratically without restricting individual autonomy.

## Rural versus Urban Applications

Turnbull commented that while CLTs have been directed towards establishing self-sufficient rural communities, which become self-sufficient through their own produce, the CLB proposals have been restricted entirely to urban development. The CLB concept was devised as a socially acceptable and financially practical way of capturing and utilizing the "windfall" gains of development. CLBs could, however, also be used in rural situations similar to those in which CLTs have been used in North America.[1]

In response, Robert Swann confirmed that CLTs have largely been associated with rural rather than urban land. This is primarily due to the fact that the impetus in the United States (and in Israel) grew out of social movements concerned with resettlement on the land. The leaders did not want to perpetuate private accumulation of wealth resulting from development by the whole community. He went on to say:

> We wanted to insure that the windfall profits in land values accrue to the community which created them, not to the individuals who did not. We in the U.S. adopted the leasehold mechanism from Israel because it seemed best suited and traditionally acceptable in rural areas. I think this mechanism is generally more suitable in rural areas than the CLB share concept, simply because farmers and rural people are not accustomed to thinking in terms of land cooperatives. (Marketing or consumer coops are, of course, an acceptable concept in rural areas.)

Swann agreed, however, with Turnbull's point that a way is needed for market forces to indicate through the pricing mechanism the value of community property, and he was interested in further considering the key money or joining fee suggestion.

On the question of applying the CLT concept to urban areas, Swann said he was unsatisfied with achievements so far. He felt that "urban people are more likely to be able to understand and accept the cooperative share concept" involved in CLBs.

However, efforts to apply the CLT concept in a city context continue. The Institute for Community Economics (which pioneered the Community Land Trust movement in North America) is seeking partnerships between urban CLTs and private developers with social concern. A person currently active in the Institute, Chuck Matthei, commented on this kind of initiative as follows:

> Through the partnership, we can purchase large low-income housing projects which have gone into default to the city or federal government. (There are tens of thousands of units in such projects across the country.) We can rehabilitate them with a lot of tenant involve-

---

[1]On the other hand, where the objective is not just self-sufficiency but the production of major economic surpluses, the value of the land (residential shares) will be determined by many interacting factors. The creation, in such a situation, of an equitable, efficient, self-correcting, and self-sustaining social and economic system is a task of quite a different order of difficulty and complexity.

ment in the planning, rehabilitation, and management processes (a specific legal economic arrangement guarantees the tenants' role in planning with the partnership), and eventually transfer them to co-operative tenant ownership (of the buildings) and CLT ownership (of the land). . . . The advantage of such an approach is that it gives tenants and trusts access to the financial and legal skills and resources of the private developer (who makes a "reasonable" return on his investment and effort), while still vesting real control over the development and management of the community.

Commenting on Turnbull's assumption that rural CLTs were aimed at "establishing self-sufficient rural communities which become self-supporting from their produce," Swann said that was not at all the intention behind the CLT movement. He agreed that a greater degree of independence or self-reliance would be desirable, especially in a region like New England, which is 85 percent dependent on food from California and elsewhere. CLTs, because they can help to provide access to land for young farm families and lower land prices generally, could reduce dependency of and vulnerability of a region like New England. However, he stressed that this is quite different from "self-sufficient rural communities."

## Size of Cooperative Land Banks: Geographical Area of Windfall Profits

Comment by Jubal Stucki:

It seems to me that when and if a CLB is ever put into operation -- and I hope we can help it happen -- it will most likely be in a neighborhood as opposed to a community. I think it is slightly optimistic that the neighborhoods will be as large as 5,000 people but I would hope they could be even larger than that eventually. It seems that the windfall profits belong to a much larger geographical area than most neighborhoods or even communities. At least some types of windfall profits belong to a much larger society, and giving them all to the neighborhood is only a slight improvement over letting individuals in the neighborhood put them into their own pocket.

One possible solution to this may be a regional Land Bank Cooperative that operates local branches. This may be a partial solution in that a portion of the land rent may go to the regional coop and the local coops may have boards with representatives from the regional coop or from other local coops.

In land trusts, we have tried to differentiate between a private trust -- owned and controlled by residents -- and community trusts, which are only partially owned and controlled by residents. We feel the Community Land Trust is highly preferable. I guess I am hoping that you would make the same sort of distinction with Land Bank Cooperatives. The Community Land Bank Cooperative may be the ultimate solution to the possessional problem, preferable even to the Community Land Trust. I personally want to start writing and talking about Community Land Bank Cooperatives.

Reply by Shann Turnbull:

I cannot but agree with the point that windfall profits could belong to an area greater than a neighborhood of 5,000 people within a large city. This would not be so with isolated towns (such as the mining communities in Western Australia).[2] In any large city, however, one part could always have some effect on the values of another part. Some degree of arbitrariness and compromise would thus always exist in dividing up a large city into CLBs.

From the information provided by town and city planners, there would seem to be natural modules into which new towns and extensions to old cities can be divided. These modules, which could contain up to around 30,000 people, arise from the school system required to support local high schools and trade schools. Geographic modules of this size were part of the design for new towns proposed by Sir Ebenezer Howard in 1898. It also corresponds to the size of the new suburbs established in Canberra over the last few years. A community of around 30,000 would seem to be suitable as a basic building block or electorate for a state and/or federal government.

I believe that the alienation which would emerge in communities larger than 30,000 could jeopardize the sense of close economic interdependence of all members within a community. Thus, while some windfall profits could still arise from outside a community of 30,000 people, I believe that these would:

- be offset by windfall profits the community contributed back to its neighboring areas;
- have little relevance to the behavior of residents. This should be the overriding criterion as the purpose of changing the rules of land ownership (land tenure system) is to accommodate the realities of human behavior in a more mutually supporting manner.

## Conditions for Making a CLT or CLB Work

Comment by Jubal Stucki:

---

[2]The CLB concept was initially developed with such communities in view.

I have come to the belief that two conditions are necessary over the long run to make a CLT or CLB work. These are that the organization must have some support and input from the outside community and that control must not be left exclusively to those who use and benefit from the land and improvements. The smaller the geographical area involved, the more important it is that some provision be made for both partial control and the division of the windfall profits outside of the neighborhood. This is a lesson we learn from history -- from some of the Georgist enclaves and the older land trusts. It seems clear that individual would rather pocket the profits than to share them and that when it is possible to do so, the individuals will seek to avoid the payment of economic rent, even to their own community cooperative.

In some cases, the avoidance of economic rent has taken the form of an unwillingness to assess themselves an adequate tax. In the case of the land bank, this would most likely take the form of much too low a discount on the shares. In some cases, it has meant that the users have decided to reduce the property to a private property system when it was to their individual advantage to do so. Any closed system, a system which is entirely controlled from within by and for the users, runs added risk that those users can and probably will change the system when it is to their advantage to do so.

I therefore strongly suggest that about one-third of the trustees should be elected from the public in general and/or from the holders of investment shares. Perhaps among a nine-person board a minority should represent the larger community and unanimous consent should be required for changes in the structure. I believe some such system is a necessity for the long-term survival of the coop.

Reply by Shann Turnbull:

I shall comment in turn on each of the two conditions proposed by Jubal:

*External (material or economic) support and input*

I do not believe that there should be a need for this condition in a CLT, while in a CLB it is important that there not be outside support. The reason why it is important for a CLB not to have outside support is that it would no longer become self-sufficient and so a self-financing closed system. It is through making a CLB a closed, independent economic entity which must pay its own way that it is forced over the long term to become internally self-correcting and self-managing through its own inbuilt checks and balances, like any national economy or individual. The basic objective of the CLB concept is to create an independent economic and political unit.

If each part of an economic system can be self-sustaining, then there will be a reduction in the need for cross subsidies and conflicts between the parts in making the whole system self-sustaining. Thus, if we can make CLBs financially independent, the problem of making their national economy financially independent is greatly reduced. The same thinking applies to individuals and their families, families and their communities, communities and their suburbs/towns or CLBs.

Economic development is not a zero sum process. Economic development in a material sense results in an overall increase in the power of a community both to produce and to consume. I believe that the great potential of CLBs to accelerate the development process in the upgrading of squatter settlements is that they provide an institutional basis for conserving and internalizing the values added by the development process back into the community creating the development, rather than allowing new development values to be drained away through traditional Western property and financial arrangements which result in making the rich richer.

I can well understand Jubal's view that a CLT must have external support and control. A CLT does not have dynamic tenure arrangements, nor even negotiable property rights, which can provide residents with new economic values according to their personal contribution in generating new values in the community by either:

- their productive effort in home and community improvements, or
- their bidding up the prices of property by their demand for rental space or home ownership.

Also, it is very difficult if not impossible to internalize the checks and balances in the management of a community when it receives external support, subsidies, and aid.

*Control of the organization not to be left to those who benefit from improvements*

I believe that the need for this condition in a CLB should be considerably less than with a CLT. The reason for my view in this regard is that one intrinsic design objective of a CLB is that there should always be conflicts of interest within the community to produce self-limiting constraints to protect its short-term and long-term viability. The more important dichotomy of conflicts arise between:

- tenants versus owner-occupiers,
- owner-occupiers versus non-resident owners,
- non-resident investors versus resident investors,
- new residents versus long-established residents,
- residents producing income versus residents dependent upon the income of others, or

- residents dependent upon others versus residents providing unpaid community services.

The balance of influence between the first four dichotomies is forced to change constantly through the dynamic tenure arrangements built into the CLB. The property tenure relationships built into the constitution of a CLB are designed to interlink with the political tenure relationship of its management to provide self-limiting and so self-managing checks and balances from within -- not from outside. This interlinking is referred to in paragraphs 18, 19, and 20 of my 1976 UN Habitat paper *Land Leases without Landlords* (see note at the beginning of Chapter 13).

Traditional Western management structures are not designed to be internally self-correcting. Indeed, they all suffer a number of fundamental flaws, which I believe justify Jubal's views. The two most crucial flaws are:

- the extent to which power is delegated and concentrated in a "pyramid" or "hierarchical" command structure in modern business and government organizations, and
- the conflict of interest created in executives by a higher level management that requires the executive to provide information on which their own actions and future tenure in the organization will be assessed.

Both flaws can be simply overcome by a separation of powers at the micro level along the lines provided by the U.S. Constitution at the macro level. Sir Ebenezer Howard had elements of this approach in the management structure he proposed for his garden cities. A more detailed development of this approach will be found described in my report on self-sufficiency, which was tabled in the Australian Parliament on November 23, 1978. I refer especially to Chapter 15, "Self-Management Structures" and Appendix 10, "Self-Correcting Self-Management."

In regard to the dynamic tenure arrangements, it should be noted that these would be built into the constitution of the CLB. To avoid exploitation of minority interests, I would agree with Jubal that it should be difficult to change the constitution. But I do not think that the constitution should be any more difficult to amend than the U.S. Constitution.

If there is any doubt about the feasibility or the practicality of internal self-management, I would like to point out that the Australian Aborigines, like the North American Indians, maintained such an arrangement in small communities for tens of thousands of years.

## Motivating People to Accept a CLB

### What If Not Enough People Join?

Robert Swann posed this question:

> Will the CLB concept work if a large number (majority) of pre-
> sent property owners will not join in?  Are there sufficient incentives
> or pressures which can be applied to bring the minimum number of
> property owners into the CLB to make it work?  What percentage
> would the minimum be?

Shann Turnbull conceded that this is a difficult question.  He said that:

> A CLB made up of non-contiguous land holdings could work in
> some situations.  Its benefits, however, could be considerably dimin-
> ished.  I analyzed such a situation for a coastal mining town in West-
> ern Australia.  The key factor in that sort of case would be to obtain
> cooperation or even outright possession of the local authorities, such
> as the Council and those providing water, sewerage, power, gas, etc.
> If control or preference could be obtained over the roads and other
> public utilities serves then, of course, the bargaining power to obtain
> greater cooperation by all could become irresistible!

### Need for an Idealistic, Quasi-Religions Commitment?

Jubal Stucki believes that people would not be able to be persuaded
to an acceptance of CLBs simply on ground of economic self-interest, in
the absence of a prior emotional or idealistic commitment.  He elabo-
rated on this point as follows:

> From the point of view of implementing the cooperative, I have
> doubts that it can or should be presented to residents or investors as
> something which will be to their short-run economic advantage.  I
> believe that people must first and foremost be convinced that it is to
> every person's long-run advantage to change the private property
> system and that it is immoral to put windfall profits into private bank
> accounts.  In this sense, the selling of the concept will take on more
> of the aspect of a "religious revival" than it will a strict dollars-and-
> sense approach.  Only in the very long run, when most of the land is
> out of the hands of private speculators, will the land bank or the land
> trust be to the direct financial benefit of all of the persons involved.
> I don't think you can liberate land from the private system without
> somebody paying the cost.  The willingness to pay that cost must

come as a result of fervent conviction. It has been my experience that this conviction of the immorality of private land ownership always precedes any concrete action, and without it, I don't know how it can be presented to any clear-thinking person. It will have economic benefits, but the social and political benefits will outweigh the economic benefits.

Here is Shann Turnbull's response:

> I do not believe that the CLBs necessarily require a religious type of commitment to gain acceptance. Development is not a zero sum process, as I noted earlier. The CLB allows everybody to become better off through the development of urban land. The CLB can thus provide a way for the majority of voters in a community to further their own economic interests in both the short term (e.g., free shares) and in the long term. The CLB could thus provide the basis for spontaneous grassroots acceptance, without the need for an idealistic approach. But for this to happen, the majority of people must obtain the knowledge of how the CLB system works and how it furthers their own self-interest in the short and long term. As Mao Tse-Tung said, "One can only create a revolution if the ordinary people can see it as in their own self-interest."

### "Free Shares" as Incentives to Join New CLBs

Jubal Stucki objected to the suggestion conveyed in the term "free shares" that there will be something for nothing.

> Extra incentives may be necessary, as you say, but I think that perhaps one should not speak of "free shares." It may be possible to phase in the coop by letting each subsequent user of a piece of real property bear part of the real cost. I doubt if it is good politics or good economics to give "free shares" to some of the early participants. Maybe I just don't fully understand the process.

Shann Turnbull responded in this manner:

> I agree that it may be unwise to refer to "free shares," but this is in fact what is intended for the pioneer home buyers who invest their savings and labor in establishing untried, new, or redeveloped residential areas. It is these people who test inconvenience or inadequate and undeveloped facilities. It is common practice for commercial property developers to subsidize the pioneer buyers in opening up a new housing estate, so it must make good business sense to subsidize pioneers.

The free shares issued to pioneer home buyers, however, do not have any immediate value to them because of the redemption discount which would apply to these charges. The redemption discount would initially be 100 percent and decline to zero over, say, a 20-year period on a continuous linear basis to create a dynamic tenure arrangement.

Such a discount would mean that a pioneer home buyer would only capture 25 percent of the value of the land on which his home is built after he had owned it for five years. The 75 percent which he did not capture would accrue to the rest of the community. As the shares redeemed would be reissued to the purchaser at a price reflecting their asset value, the community would capture a cash profit for repaying loans, set-up costs, and operating expenses. It is by this means that the CLB becomes self-financing as is analyzed in Appendix 4 in my UN Habitat paper *Land Leases without Landlords*. While all residents may not be owners, the dynamic tenure arrangements, based on a 50-year transfer rate, would provide tenants with an equity in their residence.

## Implementing the CLB and CLT Concepts

### Transfer of Title to CLB Where a Property Is Heavily Mortgaged

On this subject, the following points were raised by Robert Swann:

What happens when an owner (resident or non-resident) wants to transfer title to the CLB (in exchange for shares in the CLB), but when his equity in the property to be transferred is relatively small (10 to 20 percent or larger) with the rest held as a mortgage by a local savings bank, insurance company, etc.? Does the lending institution have to agree to the transfer? If so, will it resist? What are the problems and possibilities for the CLB?

Mortgages on privately owned land might actually present an opportunity for the CLB and an incentive to the landowners. In theory, at least, the CLB might be in a good position to refinance such mortgages at lower interest rates because it could "package" a very substantial block of mortgages to a single (or pool of) investment institution(s). In the U.S. recently, the Federal National Mortgage Association (FNMA) announced that it was making available a large sum (over a billion dollars) for central city mortgages at below market rates of interest as a subsidy for central city development.

Furthermore, the CLB should be able to argue for lower interest rates for such mortgages because the mortgage will be protected against the dangers of neighborhood deterioration, which concern banks and can cause them to place higher interest rates on (or redline) inner-city development.

On the other hand, in view of the present inflation and resulting higher market interest rates, it is likely that in most cases existing mortgages taken out two to ten years ago will be at lower rates than will be possible under present conditions. In these cases, if a lending institution has the legal power (and uses it) to prevent a shift in title ownership without also a shift in the mortgage, are there any options open to the CLB to attract the present landowner? (Hopefully, of course, the lending institution should be willing to accept the shift in title and assumption of mortgage by the CLB, because it can be argued that in this way its mortgage is better protected since the entire neighborhood development is made possible through the CLB.)

However, it is predictable that this would require considerable education of local savings banks and that few would be willing to be involved. One of their fears would be that larger financial institutions would be able to capture the mortgage business, simply because of the potential size of the CLB. One way to combat this fear would be for the CLB organizers to suggest to local savings banks (which, after all, do provide a real service to the community) that they should join in a pool and make block investments in the CLB.

Another approach would be for the CLB, once it is reasonably established, or even early in its development, to take on a banking function. Exactly how to do this is another question. One possibility would be to buy out, or transform, an existing savings bank into a subsidiary of the CLB. Opportunities to do this have arisen in some U.S. areas. For example, in an urban district in the South Shore area of Chicago, a local bank, pressured by a deteriorating neighborhood, agreed to sell out to a community organization. The bank has done well, with deposits much higher than at the time of takeover, its investments being made primarily in the local area.

### Sale of CLB Shares

Robert Swann posed this question:

Will resident owners of the CLB be able to sell their shares, or part of their shares, on the open market when they need cash if they are not moving out of their dwelling unit? Or does the CLB prevent the sale of stock unless or until resident/owners are actually moving out? The criticism here is that if they can sell shares without moving, won't the investor/rich buy back the assets again -- and we're back to where we started? Incidentally, one answer I have suggested is that the CLB could set a high discount rate on shares which are sold to non-residents, and could adjust the discount rate to discourage such practices.

Shann Turnbull replied:

> Residential shares in a CLB can only be sold if their associated "space" or "strata" title (i.e., the title to their dwelling) is also sold. This does not mean that the owner-occupier must move out, since he could continue as a tenant provided he paid a market rent to the new non-resident owner. The new non-resident owner would suffer an annual dilution of his equity through the dynamic tenure arrangements which transfer automatically with the passage of time ownership values from non-users to users. The dynamic tenure provides the mechanism for preventing the rich getting richer as presently occurs with static tenure systems. Instead of selling his title, a resident/owner could borrow against the value of his title if he was short of cash. Beside borrowing against his "space" title in a normal way, arrangements might be made to allow him to borrow also against his associated residential shares. The CLB itself might help in this regard.

Swann saw these safeguards against residents losing equity or control over their apartments as reasonable, as long as tenacity is protected by the contract. He wondered, however:

> If some other way should be found to limit the sale of stock at any time -- such as no more than 20 percent in a particular year. I realize my fears may be unnecessary but I would like to feel secure that we are not setting up a situation which would encourage recycling of wealth back to the rich. (This, by the way, is one of the criticisms leveled at some worker-ownership systems -- including Kelso's.)

Swann noted that the International Cooperative Association (ICA) had put forward a proposal to avoid this defect by dividing the traditional ownership share into two parts -- one for voting purposes and the other for ownership purposes. The ICA proposal was based in large part on the highly successful system of worker cooperatives at Mondragon in the Basque region of Spain.

### Practicalities of Implementation of CLBs or CLTs

Swann commented that:

> The most difficult problem in establishing a CLB or a CLT is

initiating the process for property acquisition, managing the property, and maintaining the dynamic for acquisition until at least most of the property in a defined area belongs to the CLB corporation.

He suggested that a "planning charrette" might be a good vehicle for initiating a CLB or CLT:

> Basically, a planning charrette is a community process, a series of events (public meetings, workshops, etc.) which lasts over a period of two to six months, and increasingly attempts to involve more and more people in the community in the process. It begins as an open-ended discussion with many different ideas and proposals being presented, sometimes by experts, sometimes by community people. The objective is to arrive at a community consensus. The charrette begins slowly but increases in intensity as it reaches the final stage -- sometimes ending with three or four days of continuous intensive meetings. The effort is to get commitment from the widest possible segment of a community. In the U.S., the process has been developed over the last ten years to something of a "fine art" and foundations and government agencies have funded most of the costs (usually $10,000 to $20,000 for the cost of coordination, consultants, etc.).

# Chapter 15

# WORLD RESOURCES TRUSTEESHIP

## Robert Swann

*Land trusts in their various forms represent concrete ways, at the local community level, of addressing what is in fact a global problem -- that of wise stewardship of the world's natural resources. Here Robert Swann provides an encompassing framework for addressing that question, building upon the land trust movement in the U.S. and comparable efforts in other countries.*

If we look at the question of natural resources form a world perspective, most people will agree in theory that, ideally, such resources as oil, gas, and minerals, for instance, should be held under a trusteeship for all the people of the world, allocated and used in such a way as to distribute equitably their use with a planned phaseout as other sources (such as solar energy) are made available for use. For example, if a world trusteeship were presently holding oil and gas, the two major sources of energy, it could lease their exploitation (at prices to control unearned profit) to private or public corporations for drilling and selling, and use the lease income to promote, research, and develop alternative sources of energy such as solar. In this fashion, the concept of the Community Land Trust could be applied on a world level to all natural resources.

Lest anyone suppose that this is a purely theoretical problem, consider the debate which has been going on over the so-called "Law of the

Seas" for several years, over the issue of who (what countries, corporations, etc.) are going to control exploitation of the rich mineral resources on the bottom of the oceans. Clearly, no country can claim "sovereignty" over the middle of the Atlantic or Pacific Oceans.

It is true that the issue would not have arisen except for the fact that new technology has made such exploitation possible. But it is also true that, if such technology had been available to the "big" countries several years ago, it is likely that they would not have waited for an international agreement before going ahead with exploitation. In fact, the U.S. and other countries have been threatening to go ahead in any case. What is important is that so far they have been restrained, even though the Reagan Administration says that it does not consider U.S. companies inhibited by the "Law of the Sea" agreement that was finally negotiated after years of effort.

Why have they been restrained? Perhaps the most plausible answer may be that there exists today a worldwide consciousness of the moral issue involved in such unilateral exploitation and even the big countries feel constrained by this consciousness. It is also true, of course, that within the United Nations, where the debate is taking place, the number and role of the less powerful countries has grown significantly in recent years so that, in number at least, they play an increasingly important role. But it was not many years ago that such considerations of unilateral action were no deterrent to the big countries when their own interests were involved.

If we can agree that while the world may be moving slowly towards a world trusteeship of natural resources, the real problem is how can it move more rapidly in that direction, and, more specifically, how can the present land trust movement contribute toward this direction. Clearly, the educational value of CLTs and their impact at a local level is part of the process which must go on. This educational process, however, may be greatly enhanced, if there exists an organic relationship between local Community Land Trusts and the resources which they possess and the development of a world trusteeship of resources. The purpose of this chapter is to explore how this might come about.

In the first place, every local Community Land Trust possesses certain potentially valuable mineral resources which it withholds from the lease rights it designates to leaseholders. These mineral rights could, in theory at least, become very valuable if oil, gas, or coal, for instance, should be discovered beneath the land held by a CLT. While this may seem a remote possibility, it is not beyond imagination as CLT holdings increase around the world. However, perhaps the most important consideration, or the consideration of most immediate consequence, is natural forests. How should such forests be treated? Should they be treated as natural resources which Community Land Trusts hold for the common good (as mineral resources are) or should they be considered the sole possession of the leaseholder and for his/her use and purposes only?

Clearly, this is an important question because probably more than 50 percent of all the land which is being acquired by CLTs, at least in the Northeastern United States, consists of natural forests.

I would argue that these grown forests should be treated as natural resources, since they generally grew through natural regeneration or were planted by other people -- certainly not the leaseholders who now occupy the land. (This does not mean that they should not be used by the leaseholders in the same way that the leaseholder uses topsoil, a natural resource, for farming in return for payments of the lease.) The Community Land Trust's role is first to protect the forests from being misused, in the same way its role is to protect the topsoil from being misused and lost.

But, unlike the topsoil, which only the individual farmer can use and plant, the forests represent a unique problem. The best management of the forestland, partly because of the nature of forests themselves and partly because forests take more than one generation to grow and produce, can be accomplished only on a broader community basis. Thus, the forests represent a resource for the whole community. This has long been recognized in most parts of the world where forests are often held as "town forests," or at the state and national level as resources for public recreation, wildlife preservation, as well as for firewood or lumber resources.

Generally, good professional forest management becomes possible only when fairly large acreages of forestland can be managed as a unit. This is due to several reasons, but primarily it is because individual landowners (or users) are not skilled or knowledgeable regarding the complexity of forest management, particularly sustained yield management, which requires a sophisticated knowledge of many species of trees, their use, value, and role in the forest ecology. Moreover, considering the relatively low return per acre on forest production and the long-term perspective required (compared with farming), it does not pay a farmer, or small woodlot owner, to spend his/her time studying and learning all of the intricate ecology and economics which foresters spend years in school learning.

A landowner or land user may, of course, hire a professional forester or have a state paid forester advise him/her on the management of his/her forestland. In fact, however, this seldom happens because it is either too expensive to hire a professional for the small size of a woodlot, or because state foresters are either unavailable or when they do advise, their advice alone is inadequate to maximize utilization and protection of the forest as a resource.

For all of these reasons, management of forestland as a resource should become the responsibility of the Community Land Trust. It is in the position (once its acquisitions are large enough) to hire very competent foresters to manage on a continued, sustained-yield basis all of the forests, or woodlots, which it has acquired and will acquire in the future. My contention is that only in this way can both the maximum utilization and the protection of this natural resource be maintained for the present as well as future generations.

Presently, due to our problems of small private ownership, the forestland is the most underutilized (or improperly utilized) of all natural resources in the United States. (In New England only about 5 percent of the forests are under management.) Except in some European countries, I suspect this is true on a worldwide basis. This is not the place to elaborate on the importance of forests as a worldwide resource and the growing danger which presently exists in many so-called developing countries of the loss or erosion of forestland due in large part to increasing population and demand for firewood.[1] So far, this danger has not existed in the United States, but with the pressure of the "energy crisis" and the growing demand for paper, lumber, and other forest products, it will in the future become increasingly important and more difficult to protect the forestland against rapacious cutting. Community Land Trusts can and should play an important role in preventing this from happening.

Therefore, I would suggest that Community Land Trusts establish the use factor of forestland in the price of the leasehold, which would permit all leaseholders to cut firewood within the framework of a Forest Management which the CLT provides, but only to the extent of the leaseholder's needs for his/her own heating purposes, etc. (During the early years of CLT establishment, before a management plan has been worked out, the CLT would permit selective cutting on the basis of advice from state foresters, if possible.)

Revenues, then, from forestry management, logging, etc. would accrue to the CLT to help cover its operating cost and to develop a land acquisition fund for further land acquisition. Some portion of this revenue, however, should be set aside for the development of a World Resources Trusteeship Fund, just as we were postulating that oil lease revenues should be held by a World Resources Trusteeship for the benefit of the population as a whole. Thus, we can see in outline the possibility for an organic relationship between local Community Land Trusts' natural resources (primary forests) and the beginning of a World Resources Trusteeship.

The most difficult question is how could, or should, such a World Resources Trusteeship be constructed or developed. To sketch in an outline, it would be useful, probably from the very beginning, to try to utilize the principles which we have tried to use in constructing the local boards of Community Land Trusts and the regional networks. Initially, of course, at the local level board members of the CLTs are essentially self-appointed and to some degree self-perpetuating, since a constituency does not exist. As local organizations grow and a constituency develops this

---

[1]See Erik Eckholm, *Losing Ground: Environmental Assets in World Food Prospects* (Elmsford, New York: Pergamon Press, 1978) for documentation.

constituency has a vote, usually according to the by-laws of local CLTs.

However, in order to create a network of experienced board members and to provide an objective viewpoint to the local situation, we have recommended that some board members (perhaps one-third) should come from a wider regional area and be persons with some experience, hopefully, to contribute. We also suggest that professionals, or local officials who have some special skills (legal, land use planning, architectural, and so forth) should be invited on the board (also one-third) in order to create as balanced a board as possible.

Applying this concept to a worldwide trust, we could invite individuals around the world with the widest experience in land and trusteeship. One thinks of Vinoba Bhave or J.P. Narayan in India, while they were alive, or Lanzo Del Vasta in France, and perhaps Julius Nyere in Tanzania. Included might be some key members of the UN -- particularly those working on the "Law of the Seas" problem, such as Elizabeth Mann-Borghese or others involved with global resources (of the stature of Buckminster Fuller, were he still alive). Perhaps, initially, these "elder statesmen" would have an honorary position, while the working members of the trust would be selected or appointed by local or regional groups.

While all of this may seem relatively far off and visionary, I want to point out several factors which would make it much more practical than it might at first seem. I have often observed to local groups that one important reason for setting up a non-profit Community Land Trust is simply because without such a local organization, gifts of land (or money to purchase land) have no place to go. And if this seems idealistic, consider the facts: a quarter of a century ago, the Nature Conservancy was established as a private agency to receive gifts of land (or money to purchase land) which needed to be protected for special ecological reasons. Since then, millions of dollars and thousands of acres of valuable land have been given to or bought for the Conservancy to be set aside for these reasons.

It is not at all inconceivable that as Community Land Trusts grow in significance an increasing number of landowners and contributors will provide the bulk of CLT land as gifts. (One of the Nature Conservancy directors once told me that we should get "all the land we need" as a gift to Community Land Trusts.) We are working on a number of ways to facilitate and encourage such giving (with advantages to landowners also), which already amounts to thousands of dollars in land and money.

One major obstacle to such gifts has been the reluctance of the IRS to grant tax deductible status to local CLTs. Nevertheless, the IRS will grant deductability for gifts which are natural resources for conservation, including forests. For this reason, we have established the American Natural Resources Trust, which like the Natural Conservancy can receive gifts of land, including farmland, but is permitted to retain only the natural resources (mainly forestland). Thus, gifts of land (some have already been received), of which the American Natural Resources Trust retains only the forestland, would be put into long-range forest management (probably managed by the local CLT), while the farmland would be conveyed to local CLTs, and the revenues from the forestland would be put into the World Resources Trusteeship Fund. But since the land had been given without purchase cost, the ANRT should be able to add revenues to the World Resources Trusteeship Fund more rapidly than land purchased by local Community Land Trusts.

But most important, it needs to be pointed out that in order to encourage such gifts of land, the entire CLT movement must be strengthened in such a way that potential land donors perceive that at a local, national, and even world level, the movement consists of responsible trustees and has a structure that provides the greatest possible stability and long-range continuity. Hence, the importance of an integrated structure and of well-known, reputable persons as national or world trustees.

How would revenues to a world trusteeship be expended? This, of course, would be a decision for the world trustees. But we could speculate that first priority would be the long-range viability of the forestland already held. This would mean assurance of the best management and use of the forests. Second, would be acquisition of additional holdings on a world basis wherever the need (for forestation and protection) exists and wherever CLTs exist or could be developed (India, for example). Also important would be general education about forest conservation and use of the trusteeship principle with the objective of increasingly including other natural resources in the holding of the World Resources Trusteeship (oil and gas), increasing pressure through education to take such resources out of private or national holdings and place them in the World Resources Trusteeship, and providing funds for research or work on other alternative energy sources (particularly solar energy).

A further note needs to be added here to underline the importance of land as a gift or gift money to purchase land. The point is simply this: in its widest or deepest concept, the Community Land Trust movement is designed to reduce the cost of land or the cost of access to land towards zero, or as close to zero as possible. This does not mean that the yearly leasehold charge should be reduced to zero. The lease is the individual's payment to society for the use of land and resource which are limited and cannot be equitably distributed in any other way. Land, which was originally given without cost by God or nature, should be returned to society (the general welfare) without the addition of a price, which as Henry George pointed out represents "unearned increment." Thus, gifts of land (or money) have a very important economic role, and should be treated as a partial return to nature or God, the spiritual part of humankind from which it originally came.

Such an attitude or feeling about land is very widely felt among human beings and was clearly expressed by native Americans, indeed native people all over the world, before the commercial spirit of the "industrial revolution" overtook Western civilization in the last 200 years. But the original spirit remains in many people and today we see it manifest in different ways. We must not ignore this spirit as the classical (and Marxist) economists have done and assume that land must be sought and paid for as a community or taken forcibly away from individuals and placed in the hands of the state. For it is on this spirit, this instinctive need to protect and care for land that resides deep inside all of us, it is on this spirit which the future of the human race depends -- gradually returning land to its original place in economics, a gift from God or nature.

# COMMUNITY SELF-MANAGEMENT

# Chapter 16

# SOCIAL CAPITALISM AS THE ROAD TO COMMUNITY SELF-MANAGEMENT

*Shann Turnbull*

We are faced with the interlocking collapse of our systems of employment, ownership of wealth, taxation, and means of production. And we are compounding this by rapidly becoming satiated, so there is less and less demand for the goods produced by more and more machines.

What is required is a new social order. To arrive at it we need new patterns of thinking. The accepted or conventional wisdoms of our time have demonstrably failed us. But new thought patterns, or paradigms, are being bitterly resisted by conventional economists who have a vested interest in maintaining the status quo.

I believe the answer lies in a plan which I will call for want of a better title social capitalism. Social capitalism would introduce in rich and poor countries a golden age of a decentralized, self-reliant, humane, and ecological society. It involves sharing ownership (in negotiable terms of an investment trust), no taxation, and new patterns of work and income distribution. It would make irrelevant the present obsessions of governments in industrial societies with the unemployment rate. Policies for full employment would be replaced with policies of fulfillment of employment.

The picture of society under social capitalism sketched here is, of course, a visionary one, and I have no doubt yesterday's men who hold the reins of power today will challenge or dismiss it. But I am in good company with others whose ideas were dismissed at first as "visionary." No one listened in the beginning to Copernicus, Darwin, or Pasteur.

Today's world is at a turning point, and the options, particularly for the Western world, are limited. The only way these countries with their market economies can avoid increasing taxation and government intervention without resorting to state ownership of the means of production is to adopt social capitalism. This would solve the income distribution problem without taxation by distributing the ownership of the assets which produce income. Income is provided to the unemployed simply by allowing the workers to own the machines which put them out of work.

Economists have not seriously considered this starkly simple solution to the chronic and endemic income redistribution problem created by technological unemployment because it requires changing the system. Amazingly, this is not usually considered to be part of economics. In any event, changing the system requires detailed practical knowledge of how the real world works.

Many economists will now admit that they are no longer certain of how to manage existing market economies. They agree a new system is required but they keep on trying to do the impossible because their professional training, experience, and conditioning have not prepared them to do otherwise. Indeed, the thought patterns of contemporary economists make it much more difficult for them than for others to understand the simple, practical solutions provided by social capitalism.

Social capitalism creates a major intellectual blockage for economists. It creates a radically new type of economic system which is quite different from capitalism, socialism, or communism. Social capitalism is unique because it does not use the public sector for redistributing a nation's income. Not only is social capitalism beyond the experience of economists, but it introduces quite new thought patterns and methods of analysis on how the world works.

The framework of analysis for social capitalism is the capitalist paradigm, while the framework used by conventional economists is the socialist paradigm. I refer to the latter framework as a socialist paradigm because orthodox economists in all countries simply do not consider the option of redistributing national income through redistributing the ownership of capital assets. Why should they? The communists and socialists are ideologically committed to public sector transfers.

In Western or market economies, the redistribution of national income through the private sector is not significant, and until Louis Kelso developed Employee Share Ownership Plans (ESOPs) 20 years ago, there was no practical method for entertaining an alternative to public sector transfers. The fact that even many right wing professional economists are intellectually locked into a socialist framework of analysis illustrates the power of a paradigm to create mental blockages.

The problems facing us must be seen in context. The technological revolution has no geographic or ideological constraints. It provides threats and opportunities to every soul on the planet, weak or powerful.

Because of machines, the time spent not working at one's job in industrialized societies has doubled since the last century. A 72-hour or longer working week has been replaced with a 35-hour week with less weeks worked per year and less years worked per lifetime. Even though the hours worked per person in industrialized societies have more than halved, the goods and services produced per person have increased by around 100 times.

The power of new technology to reduce work and increase output is growing at an accelerating rate. The robot revolution into that we are just entering will produce machines which will put both men and machines out of work. By the end of this century, the work rate could halve again in some countries. If the present working week were maintained, then this would create a 50 percent unemployment or "leisure rate."

This leisure rate is now being accelerated by the emergence of quite a new global phenomenon of satiation. This occurs when consumers obtain more income than they wish to spend on food, clothing, shelter, and other goods and services. As a result, consumer demands do not increase sufficiently to keep labor and machines fully employed.

The affect of technology on satiation can be seen in the television industry. Once valve-operated black and white TV sets cost $1,000. Today, with miniaturization and printed circuits, the much more complex color sets cost half as much. And because almost every home, at least in the industrialized world, has one, the TV electronic industry has to try to create a demand for something new, like video-cassette recorders.

Satiation also occurs when people change their values. Instead of seeking conspicuous consumption and possessions, they may turn to more spiritual satisfactions or those which conserve the environment. Satiation can be created as well by the ability of societies to produce excess goods and services or by obtaining excess income. Increases in productivity created by new technology are more and more providing the means for individual countries like Germany and Japan to produce more than they wish to consume. Other people and countries are becoming satiated from owning scarce natural resources that provide them with income in excess of their need to consume. The Arab oil states provide not only the best example of this situation, but an outstanding illustration of the international economic turmoil which is created when the value of imports and consumption of a country cannot match the value of its production and exports. All three forms of satiation have emerged together during the 1970s and continued in the 1980s.

Another economic problem created by the technological revolution arises from the concentration of wealth in market economies. Typically, less than 10 percent of the population own around 90 percent of all income-producing assets.  Owner-occupied homes should not be counted as an income-producing asset.  In practice, they represent an income-absorbing asset as they require repair and maintenance and may take many years to be paid off.  As a result, people need wage employment to keep their homes, whereas income-producing assets would help to support their owners and thus to keep their homes.

Because so few people typically own most of the machines, factories, mines, and other assets that produce goods and services, income distribution is also highly concentrated.  Taxation is then required to transfer income to the majority of consumers so that they can obtain sufficient money to pay for the goods and services produced by the enterprises owned by the minority.  A higher rate of taxation is required on both humanitarian grounds to provide a survival income for the unemployed and for the practical reason of providing consumers with the money to pay for the goods and services produced by the new machines.

Trying to solve this problem through higher and higher levels of taxation soon becomes self-defeating.  High levels of taxation not only encourage tax avoidance but reduce the incentive for individuals to become employed productively and for investors to risk their money in developing more productive technology.  But improvements in technology continue to emerge.  This is gradually forcing market economies into a crisis which could result in either a breakdown of the existing system or a breakthrough to a different system.

In the affluent industrialized or resource-rich societies, social capitalism will allow private wealth in the form of income-producing assets to replace public welfare.  Sufficient private assets would be provided to all adults so that they would obtain a minimum income or "social dividend" as a birthright.  This would allow a fee to be charged for all basic needs and services, thereby eliminating the need for government health, education, social, and other services.  It would also eliminate the need for big government and most taxes, which would substantially increase the income available from private assets and so the social dividend.

The private income available to all adults would allow them to buy the health, education, and other services of their choice from locally owned and managed enterprises.  These would provide a diversity and quality of service most appropriate to the locale.  But, more important, the social dividend would avoid the need for people to work to support themselves.  People could afford to work for reasons other than just obtaining money if they so wished.  The difference between work and leisure would become blurred or meaningless as people sought employment to further their natural aptitudes and interests or their drive for recognition, power, status, and influence.  Thus, the unemployment rate would be referred to as the "leisure rate."  Advances in technology would be welcomed as a means of increasing both the level of the social dividend and the "leisure rate."

But the thought of virtually eliminating taxes is so radical that it is not seriously considered by political leaders and economists in the Western world.  Indeed, it is considered to be the wishful thinking of fanatic right-wing profiteers, or simple and impractical ideologists who wish to revert to an unsophisticated primitive society.  Taxes on incomes and profits, rather than on expenditures, are in fact a relatively recent innovation of market economies.  The first income tax was introduced in England in 1798 to finance the war against France and was repealed after Waterloo.  Taxes on incomes and profits did not become a significant source of revenue until the First World War, government finance being principally based on such expenditure-type taxes as tariffs and excise.

The only advanced industrialized societies not to introduce taxes are the socialist and communist countries.  In such countries, the surplus income accrues directly to the government because it owns most of the means of production.  This illustrates the practicality in social capitalism virtually eliminating taxes as the surplus income of production is distributed by ownership sharing.  The ownership sharing is achieved in the private sector on a highly decentralized and pluralistic basis, instead of a centralized monolithic government basis.

Social capitalism is radically different from socialism or communism because it is based on this decentralized and popular-voting system of political and economic power.  The power is based on private property, rather than on monopoly centralized state ownership.  The power of private property to motivate people to produce and maintain their environment is dramatically illustrated in the Soviet Union where more than 60 percent of primary production is obtained from 3 percent of the land which is privately owned.  As well, the 55 percent ratio of private home-owners in the Soviet Union is higher than the ration of homeowners in the United States, which is around 45 percent.  The low ratio of the United States is created through the concentration of private wealth.  In the Soviet Union, the costs of repairing and maintaining residential units is so high that the government has instigated programs to promote private home ownership.  Toward this end, the government provides 15-year loans at only 3 percent interest.

The reaction against centralized bureaucratic control in the non-capitalist world has moved countries such as Yugoslavia toward a decentralized society based on a popular system of self-managing social, economic, and political units.  However, the trend in the Western world is in the opposite direction with increasing centralization of power in the hands of big government, big business, and big labor.

Rather than wait for a massive breakdown of our present market economies, we could start to create the basic building blocks of social capitalism within the present system.  These building blocks should be created quite unilaterally by different groups of people in different places, at different times, in different ways, for different purposes.  Alternatively, regional, state, and national governments could provide incentives for the voluntary transformation of existing institutions to follow the principles of social capitalism. Both approaches are already occurring in the United States.

The unilateral process was initiated 25 years ago when Louis Kelso devised a way within existing U.S. legislation for employees to purchase their employer from pre-tax profits. During the last few years, the U.S. government has introduced a number of fiscal and monetary incentives to encourage the development of "Employee Share Ownership Plans" (ESOPs).

Knowledge of the theory and practice of social capitalism is very limited. One of those who has written extensively about it is Louis Kelso, more widely known as the "father of ESOPs." He has written many articles and three books: *The Capitalist Manifesto*, *The New Capitalists*, and *The Two Factor Theory -- The Economics of Reality* (see the Bibliography at the end of this book). Kelso uses the term "universal capitalism" in his writings. During his visit to Australia in 1975, he agreed that social capitalism was a more appropriate name.

My proposals, which complement and extend the Kelso concepts to urban land and natural resources, are outlined in my book, *Democratising the Wealth of Nations* (see the Bibliography). This book was written exactly 200 years after the founding father of economics, Adam Smith, wrote his book, *An Inquiry into the Nature and Causes of the Wealth of Nations*.

My book proposes three complementary methods to the ESOPs and Consumer Share Ownership Plans (CSOPs) proposed by Kelso. All three methods are based on changing the rules by which people own things. These new rules would create new economic structures which I have referred to as Ownership Transfer Corporations, Cooperative Land Banks, and Producer-Consumer Cooperatives (see Chapters 13, 14, and 20).

The rules by which people own assets are made by man and so can be changed by man. The present widely adopted rules for owning natural resources like land and minerals or corporate assets have two fundamental defects. One common, but by no means universal, defect is that perpetual ownership rights are provided. Such perpetual monopoly claims not only deny the ability of market forces to make changes in the allocation of resources, but they can provide an excessive economic benefit.

Surplus profits are inconsistent with the operation of a market economy that assumes that profits are limited by competition. But surplus profits are more the rule than the exception. It can be said that all venture capitalists who obtain ownership rights over corporations and natural resources in excess of 20 years and obtain revenues after this period are receiving surplus profits. This is because venture capitalists like everyone else cannot accurately predict the future or the size of any future surplus of profits.

The remittance of surplus profits not only represents a bad business deal but a bad deal for the host country. In fact, all foreign operations in any country which remit any dividends after 20 years are providing surplus profits. In all such cases, the host countries are paying more than they should for foreign technology and enterprise. It is by this means that the rich nations of the world get richer at the expense of the poor.

The mechanisms of wealth concentration are rarely examined by current methods of economic analysis. The modern tools of economic analysis are as rough and useful as a sundial for measuring a 100-meter sprint record. What they do examine they are unlikely to measure, and what they do not measure they are unlikely to recognize as a serious problem. The result is the very high concentration in the ownership of productive assets -- concentration that has not been abated or even ameliorated by high levels of taxation.

Surplus profits introduce the need for more taxation so that purchasing power can be distributed to consumers to keep the economy operating. In many situations, consumers may be directly responsible for increasing the economic values of owning an asset beyond that anticipated by the owner. These unexpected values are windfall profits, the second major problem created by the present rules used for owning things.

This increase in value is not created by the owners but by the non-owners or consumers. If the consumers create these new values, should they not share in them according to how they contributed to the increase? Such a result could be produced by adopting a dynamic form of ownership which transfers ownership rights from the venture capitalists to the consumers, who generate the values of ownership in excess of its development cost. The concept of dynamic ownership rights not only minimizes the emergence of surplus profits but provides a means to distribute windfall profits.

The basic needs of all are fulfilled through providing a guaranteed minimum income. This allows people to work for fulfillment, rather than the need for a living income. Individuals obtain more than the minimum income according to their "contributions" to either production or consumption.

The present system, which is based on outmoded concepts of ownership and income distribution, helps to explain why consumers, who far outnumber the owners of the means of production, obtain such a thin slice of a nation's income cake -- an imbalance that is reaching a critical position with advancing technology. The introduction of new technology and the robot revolution will thus make social capitalism the inevitable economic system of the post-industrial age.

# Chapter 17

# ECONOMIC
# BEHAVIOR AND
# SELF-MANAGEMENT:
# SOME GOVERNING
# PRINCIPLES

*C. George Benello*

Social relations of different kinds induce various forms of economic behavior. Particularly conducive to self-management are those social relations growing out of or based upon a sense of community. During wartime the line between voluntarism and paid work becomes indistinct; people put in long hours and do what must be done. An economic crisis could bring on similar behavior. On the other hand, the market ideology -- for that is what governs our approach to economic transactions today -- conceives of human nature as primarily passive, only moved to action when a need must be met, responding to a calculus of pleasure within an overall context of self-interest. People are defined as passive consumers, casting their vote in the market in a fashion similar to their behavior in the political arena, where they also vote on prepackaged products that they have little hand in shaping.

Where relations are determined by self-interest, there is need for a supporting structure of rules buttressed by sanctions in order to assure that self-interest does not become social pathology. Economic transactions must be codified by contracts, must be overseen by watchdog agen-

cies, must be registered, stored, interpreted, insured, and periodically renewed and redefined. All of this brings with it a large cost in the form of
resources used: courts, lawyers, agencies at every level of government. It
may well be that as much or more energy goes into defining and monitoring economic activities as goes into the activities themselves.

Up to a certain point, routinization is a time and energy saver: there
are forms for mortgages, partnerships, incorporation, and the like, and if
one understands the form, often a lawyer is unnecessary. Moreover,
where a community exists, in the sense of persons with an ongoing face-
to-face experiencing of each other, relations of trust develop, and the
formalities of contractual relations can be overlooked: a handshake is as
much assurance as is needed. Within such a community, sanctions exist
without an elaborate legal and penal apparatus. To the extent that people's identities are tied to their community -- to the extent that it represents a primary group for them -- the community has power to exert social pressure to assure conformity to its norms. It operates thus by social
pressure and social norms, rather than by formal laws and punishment.

It may clarify the thrust of the argument here to construct a sort of
hierarchy of behaviors (analogous to the one Anatol Rapaport used in his
book *Fights, Games, Debates*).[1] At the lowest level, we have economic
behavior which is based on the rule of force: goods are seized, and service is enforced through slavery. At the next level up, we have the market
of the classical economists: there is "pure" competition, based on the laws
of supply and demand, with a minimum of regulation. However, for this
to operate there must exist a society where the social bond exists and is
expressed through common norms which are generally followed (as
Polanyi has shown in *The Great Transformation*).[2] If the social bond is
weak, then the pursuit of self-interest becomes unrestrained: shoddy
goods are produced, the powerful coalesce into oligopolies and gouge
consumers, trade is controlled and restricted.

An adequate treatment of the market system would take pages. But
its contradictory character derives from the fact that it assumes a considerable degree of common assent to norms, while it is at the same time
based on competition which assumes self-interest as the guiding principle.[3] Markets exist quite extensively throughout primitive societies, and it
is likely that pricing is not dependent on what the traffic would bear but
on commonly accepted conventions. In the existing system in advanced
industrial societies, the market is constrained both by a considerable degree of oligopoly, and also by external regulations governing the character

---

[1]Anatol Rapoport, *Fights, Games, Debates* (Ann Arbor: University of Michigan
Press, 1960).
[2]Karl Polanyi, *The Great Transformation* (New York: Farrar & Rinehart, 1944).
[3]For a critique of self-interest and the presentation of an alternative view of economic behavior, see Mark A. Lutz and Kenneth Lux, *Humanistic Economics: The New
Challenge* (New York: The Bootstrap Press, 1988).

and quality of goods and services.

The type of economic transactions discussed here may be termed paraprimitive. They represent at least partially a reversion to a pre-market model where, because transactions are direct and between people motivated by a considerable degree of common purpose, the formalization of contract, external supervision, third parties, and the like can be dispensed with. In this context, pricing will not be a function solely of supply and demand or what the traffic will bear, but will also include ability to pay and the financial condition of the buyer. Where barter and exchange obtains, people derive not only economic benefit but social benefit from the interaction. The principle of doing a neighbor a good turn exists, and this constitutes a kind of credit, since when there is need, the favor will be returned.

The savings in such a system derive from a number of sources. Most obviously, there is not the superstructure of third parties, supervision, and legal requirements, with the consequent involvement of lawyers, government agencies, and courts. Also, financing for such transactions does not require recourse to banks or other formal and usually distant financial institutions, but can be structured flexibly to accommodate to the situation. If neighbors are enlisted to help build a barn, the favor will be returned, and the criterion is the general reliability of the person asking the favor -- whether he in turn is likely to pitch in when someone else needs help. And, since social as well as economic benefit is derived from the transaction, pricing will reflect this. Pricing will also reflect that fact that if people respect the local mechanic or woodcutter as much as the local lawyer or doctor, the latter cannot charge hourly fees many times that of the former even though in the external market their services could bring such prices.

Urban environments tend to be places where transactions are mainly between people who have no personal acquaintance. These are environments where the controls of peer pressure are lacking, people are free to gouge, dispense shoddy goods and services, control the market, and so on. Hence, the existing superstructure of controls is necessary. But in conditions where community exists, the classical market demands for maximum economic gain are tempered and modified by the need to follow the norms of the community. Social criteria rather than purely financial criteria will be the determining factor. The necessary condition for a paraprimitive economy to work is that there be a community such that economic relations take place among people who are personally known to each other, and who have personal reputations to consider. This allows for the necessary trust to develop which alone can serve as a substitute for legal and supervisory precautions.

A paraprimitive economy is rational because it is more efficient, in the sense of being more cost effective. It does not violate the principle of reciprocity upon which classical markets are based. Rather, it elevates reciprocity to another level. This level may be best described as one where, rather than economic relations taking place primarily or mainly between isolated individuals or companies, they are understood to take place within a triadic system wherein the community is always involved. In most tribal societies, the community considers that it has an obligation to maintain the well-being of its members. Where this is the norm, members of the community are never thrown back totally on their own resources and hence are motivated to engage in personal acts of assistance. This can be understood as a condition where there is a psychic surplus on which all members of the community can draw.

Where community is lacking, people are impelled to seek maximum economic gain -- well beyond what is necessary to lead a decent life -- in part as a form of substitution for needs which are not met. To quote from a previous article of mine: ". . . the Ontong Javanese call a person poor not when he is lacking in material goods but when he is lacking in the resources of shared living."[4] Recent English research has caused renewed interest in this definition of poverty. Where psychic poverty exists, the effort is to substitute material goods. This in turn gives rise to the market ideology where selfish interest prevails. But just as there is a rationality of selfish interest, so there is a rationality of psychic plenty. The paraprimitive economy featuring psychic plenty is rational in a double sense: it constitutes a coherent set of relationships guided by a set of consistent norms, and hence can be institutionalized. Second, it is more efficient and more cost effective, being free of the burden of a superstructure made necessary for the most part by the lack of trust and reciprocity.

Cooperatives, social investment funds, and self-financing systems are examples of paraprimitive economic mechanisms. By combining social and economic values, they paradoxically end up being more cost effective than systems based on unadulterated self-interest. More accurately put, these systems are potentially more cost effective. However, the organizing requirements are greater. It is easier to jail criminals than to reform them -- even though the latter is clearly more cost effective. The paraprimitive economy assumes changed attitudes and behavior on the part of those involved, and it is easier to police people than to implement the needed changes. But where the costs of unadulterated self-interest become ruinous, the basic forces of human nature may reassert themselves and more enlightened views can prevail.

---

[4]C. George Benello, "Wasteland Culture," in Peter Dreitzel, ed., *Recent Sociology*, No. 1 (New York: Macmillan, 1969).

# Chapter 18

# WORKPLACE DEMOCRATIZATION

## C. George Benello

The workplace is clearly a central element in any community. Therefore, one important dimension to achieving community self-management is democratization of the workplace. Workplace democratization covers a broad spectrum of practices affecting the workplace. These practices stretch from limited forms of workfloor participation and work humanization programs, to Quality of Working Life programs which involve various forms of job redesign, autonomous work groups, and workfloor participation. They go on to forms of worker stock ownership and profit sharing and from there to completely democratized forms of ownership and control.

Worker participation plans may involve extensive control of the workfloor, but the term is usually contrasted with worker control or worker self-management, which denotes overall control of policy and profits. Worker ownership does not necessarily imply worker control, and there are a number of companies with employee stock ownership plans (ESOPs) which do not entail voting rights. Even with employee voting rights, control may not be democratic, since voting according to the number of shares held is different from voting on the basis of one person/one vote.

Another way of looking at the different rights involved in workplace democratization is to reduce the bundle of traditional corporate ownership rights to the following three basic rights:

- the right to vote (i.e., voting rights);
- the right to net income (i.e., profit rights);
- the right to the equity or net worth of the corporation (i.e., capital rights).

A fully democratized worker participation plan would define the first two rights -- which are membership rights attached to the functional role of working in the firm -- as *personal* rights. In a traditional "worker-capitalist" firm, these membership rights are *property* rights (e.g., a company in which most or all of the common stock is owned by the workers through an ESOP).[1] The differences between the two arrangements for worker ownership are shown in Table 1.

**Table 1**

**COMPARISON OF FORMS OF WORKER OWNERSHIP**

| Structural Comparison | Worker-Capitalist Firm | Democratic Firm |
|---|---|---|
| Hiring relation | Capital hires labor | Labor hires capital |
| Membership rights | Property rights owned by worker-shareholders | Personal rights attached to worker's role |
| Voting rights | One vote per share | One vote per person |
| Profit rights | Proportional to capital | Proportional to labor |
| Capital rights: | | |
|   Return on workers' capital | Interest plus profit rights | Interest |
|   Return on workers' labor | Wages or salaries | Wages or salaries plus profit rights |

*Source:* Adapted from David Ellerman, *Worker Ownership: Economic Democracy or Worker Capitalism?* (Somerville, Massachusetts: Industrial Cooperative Association, April 1986).

---

[1]See David Ellerman and Peter Pitegoff, "The Democratic Corporation: The New Worker Cooperative Statute in Massachusetts," *New York University Review of Law and Social Change* 11, No. 3 (1982-1983), especially p. 444.

It is important that the spectrum of workplace democratization efforts be dealt with in its entirety, since there is no evidence, at least as yet, that any part of this spectrum can be written off as either impractical or unworkable. There is evidence, at least in certain instances, that initially limited forms of participation have broadened into far more extensive forms of participation and control. Thus, while there is a fairly clear analytical division between forms of participation carried on within traditionally structured corporate enterprises and participation structured so that power is shared on the basis of one member/one vote, in practice the division is often bridged, either by firms moving from the corporate form to some form of worker ownership, or by firms which have been cooperatives selling out to corporations.

There are two sorts of perspectives favoring workplace democratization: principled and pragmatic. For the most part, the pragmatic perspective is applied to participation programs operating within the corporate system. The reasons of principle apply here as well, but are also used to evaluate worker ownership and control as part of a broader movement for social and political change, involving structural alternatives to the traditional corporate forms of control.

Thus, a workplace democratization can be seen as a movement occurring within the workplace to increase participation, but can also be seen as part of a broader movement to democratize the other major institutions of the society, such as the local community, financial institutions, state and public policy planning, and government bureaucracy. Within the workplace, the movement is not limited to private sector organizations, but applies equally to government bureaucracies, health care, education, and other public service organizations.

## Perspectives of Principle

**Arguments For**

*Ethical.* The Kantian categorical imperative states that people must always be considered as ends in themselves, never as means. For Kant, this is the basic ethical principle from which all others are derived. It means that even if one voluntarily sells one's labor to another, this does not abrogate the right or the responsibility to participate in deciding what is produced and how it is produced. Voluntary servitude is still servitude, and it violates the categorical imperative which, when applied to work, means that one cannot use another person as a tool for one's own ends. Work must be performed in freedom, through voluntary cooperation.

*Political.* The perspective here is that one cannot safely delegate one's political rights and duties to others. For if one does, *quis custodet ipsos custodes*? -- who will guard the guardians? The advocates of direct democracy -- a continuing tradition in Western political theory -- assert, in the fashion of the ethical argument, that one cannot cede one's rights of political participation any more than one can sell one's rights to participate in the control of the labor process.

Another point is that under the present system "democracy stops at the factory gate." But if democracy is to be authentic, it must apply equally to the workplace as well as to the political arena. Democratic rights cannot be arbitrarily abridged in the place one spends much of one's waking hours. When democratic rights are limited to "the public sector," the "private sector" escapes accountability and its unrestrained influence skews and limits the political democracy of the public sector.

*Psychological.* It is argued that if people are to grow into full adulthood and become responsible human beings, they must be able to make significant decisions in matters that affect their lives. In particular, people must have a chance to develop their competence and skills, and this includes both workplace and production skills, and also group process and decision-making skills -- the skills required to work effectively in a group. Motivation theory argues that workers are interested not only in monetary reward but also seek responsibility and the opportunity to develop as full human beings. Surveys indicate this to be true. Workers are motivated to participate in the control of their workplace, and will develop as human beings when this opportunity exists.

Also, there is a circular reinforcing process so that as competence is increased, greater confidence develops. This leads to a greater willingness to exercise control, leading in turn to increased competence. Just as the inability to make decisions breeds lack of confidence, so the opportunity to participate increases confidence.

*Sociological.* While organization theory often argues that coercion is an essential element in all formal, purposive-rational organizations, there is a strong counter trend represented by people such as Bennis, Argyris, McGregor, Likert, and others who argue that autonomous work groups and other non-bureaucratic forms are more effective and free of the rigidities and dysfunctions of bureaucracy.

On a more basic level, it also argues that socialization via small groups can integrate or synergize individual needs and group purposes. This experience is essential if a society of larger units that features cooperation and an egalitarian spirit is to be created. It is necessary, moreover, in order to counter the prevailing culture of individualism within contemporary society. In short, the small, task-oriented group is the basic unit for education in democratic participation. As Mary Parker Follett has argued, the small group, not the individual, should be seen as the basic unit of society.

*Economic.* An economics which recognizes the primacy of the persons and refuses to treat workers as "factors of production" will not subordinate people to profits. It will recognize that there are ecological and social implications for both what is produced and how it is produced. It also recognizes that social and ecological costs cannot be treated as externalities, the costs of which should be borne by the public. In seeking to build in a system of social accountability, such an economics will be concerned with giving a voice both to those who are involved in the work process and to those who, as members of the surrounding community or as recipients of the company's services, are most affected by its activity.

**Arguments Against**

An issue often raised concerns the practicality of democratizing the workplace. While the principled arguments for doing so may be accepted in theory, it is often asserted that it is hard or impossible in practice. Differences in aptitude, motivation, and skill level make it difficult to expect equal levels of informed participation. In the short run, it is always easier to set up an imperative organization, where decisions flow from the top down and information flows from the bottom up. It is argued that participatory decision making is often time-consuming and inefficient. Given the competition of the marketplace, firms that engage in this type of decision making will be unable to compete.

Also, it is argued that the strength of the American economic system is based on entrepreneurialism, which is a system that gives maximum freedom and incentive to the entrepreneur by allowing him/her to enjoy the fruits of his/her labor. The entrepreneur, it is argued, is the one who both makes the enterprise a reality and who takes the risks; the entrepreneur should therefore be entitled to the lion's share of the profits, and should also be the one who makes the decisions.

It is further argued that there is little in the American tradition either in business or labor that suggests a willingness to experiment with workplace democratization. Institutional systems, moreover, once evolved, are difficult to change; they become institutionalized in law, culture, and ideology. Whatever its difficulties, the present system works. Is it wise to relinquish it in favor of a system which, in this country at least, is largely untried? These are all questions which must be confronted and understood in order to be able to assess the viability of workplace democratization.

## Pragmatic Perspectives

**Arguments For**

On the pragmatic side, the position for increased participation is closely connected with the present situation in the United States, which is characterized by stagnating productivity, higher energy costs, and increased competition from abroad. The practical arguments are as follows:

It is argued that increased participation is a means to reduce labor-management conflict. Increased participation in management emphasizes the common stake that both labor and management have in increasing productivity. When unions and management are concerned with how to divide up the economic pie, their relationship is adversarial. But when productivity increases, there is more pie to divide up. Conversely, in the case of a failing enterprise, demands for increased wages may result in the loss of the business, a loss for labor as well as management.

Also, in the case of a marginal business, labor may wish to translate its traditional demands for higher wages into demands for more control, where demands of the first sort might jeopardize the business, and hence jobs.

Enhanced participation increases worker satisfaction and commitment to the job. This results in increased effectiveness, and allows workers to feel they have control over their working lives.

Increased participation reduces management and production costs in the following ways:

- In some plants where Quality of Working Life Programs have been introduced, lower level management and supervisory personnel have become redundant, thus saving labor costs.
- Suggestions by workers have saved some firms time and money and have increased productivity.
- Quality control has improved through the use of such devices as Quality Circles, and a better product has resulted with less need for external forms of quality control.

With the changes in the cultural climate that resulted from the movements of the sixties and seventies, management is coming to recognize that the old authoritarian methods of management are counterproductive. Workers today are interested in more than a paycheck; they expect a greater measure of freedom on the job. Participation programs speak to this need.

### Arguments Against

Quality of Working Life Programs and other types of participation programs have often been initiated by companies so as to prevent unionization or weaken the union movement. However, the largest Quality of Working Life programs now in place have been instigated with the cooperation of unions. The union movement has been concerned that when participation programs have been introduced at the initiative of management, the real reason has been to increase productivity. This has raised questions regarding the extent to which such programs involve any genuine sharing of power. There is the further question as to the workers' rights to share in any productivity gains that result.

Also, the initiation of participation programs has often been threatening to middle and lower management, since such programs can potentially make their jobs redundant. Yet, without the cooperation of these levels of management, participation programs usually will not work. There are reasons for management as well as unions to be suspicious of participation programs.

Finally, for those who believe the development of greater workplace democratization to be important, the question of how corporate participation programs fit can be raised. Do they represent genuine advances in the degree of workplace control and democratization, or do they represent attempts at cooptation without real empowerment?

## Personal Rights, Property Rights, and Democratization of the Workplace[2]

The vision of those who believe in a fully democratized workplace is one in which conventionally defined property rights are redefined as personal rights. This involves, in essence, extending the principles of political democracy to the economic domain.

For two centuries the United States has struggled to create a political democracy, however imperfect it may be. That form of government involves certain principles, of which the one-person/one-vote principle is one of the most important. Any design of a democratic business firm should be based on that essential principle.

Democracy is people-based, not property-based or capital-based. Democracy is thus a method for people to govern themselves, not a method for property owners to govern their property. The key question before us becomes: How can democracy be extended from the communities where people live to the communities where people work? David Ellerman, Staff Economist and one of the founders of the Industrial Cooperative Association, puts it this way:

> The voting and other citizenship rights in a democratic polity are personal or human rights, not property rights which may be bought or sold. Property rights are marketable so they can become highly concentrated in huge accumulations of wealth and power. People qualify for personal or human rights by having a certain functional role so these rights may not be "bought" or "sold.". . . For instance, the voting rights in a township or municipality are personal rights at-

---

[2]Addendum by the editor.

tached to the functional role of legally residing within the township or municipality. These rights are automatically distributed on a one per person basis. . . . People may not sell these voting rights. In any democracy, political or industrial, the basic citizenship or membership rights should be assigned as non-marketable personal or human rights, not as marketable property rights, to those who are governed.[3]

In the discourse of the eighteenth century, there are two basic "natural rights": the right of democratic self-government and the right to the fruits of one's labor. Democratization of the workplace involves structuring organizations so that the right to govern is linked to the functional role of being governed, and the membership or personal right of one worker/one vote in controlling the business firm and the rights to the fruits of the production are linked to the functional role of producing these products.

## Workplace Democratization Today

At present, there is extensive interest on the part of the corporate system in increasing participation in the workplace. There is also a growing interest in such democratic alternatives as cooperatives and worker-owned enterprises. Some of the reasons for this have already been suggested. Further reasons, which derive directly from contemporary social, economic, and cultural conditions in the United States, are also worthy of note.

From management perspective, the advanced education level of today's workforce means that workers expect to have meaningful work and expect to have a say in workplace decisions. These expectations are also a product of the movements of the sixties and seventies for greater self-determination: the civil rights movement and the student movement of the sixties, in particular, have been influential. In the seventies, the feminist movement and the consumer and ecology movements have raised issues regarding corporate policies as well as the impact of the corporation on the consumer and on the environment.

The decline of the United States from it postwar position as industrial leader of the world and the corresponding rise of foreign competition has, along with higher energy costs, placed far greater pressure on the American industrial system to perform. But American productivity has not been equal to the challenge; instead growth of U.S. productivity has

---

[3]David Ellerman and Peter Pitegoff, *Worker Ownership: Economic Democracy or Worker Capitalism?* (Somerville, Massachusetts: Industrial Cooperative Association, April 1986), p. 3.

fallen significantly below the level of its major international competitors. Costs have risen and profit margins in many cases have decreased.

As margins lessen, there is pressure to substitute other incentives beside continuous wage increases. In this situation, both labor and management have discovered they share a common interest in maintaining economic viability. The near bankruptcy of several large firms, especially in the auto industry, has forced labor and management to recognize that they have a common stake in remaining competitive. Labor's role in helping bail out these failing companies has at the same time given them greater power in overall decision making.

On the side of the unions, the response to corporate participation programs has evolved from initial suspicion and rejection to one of guarded acceptance, at least on the part of such unions as the Machinists, the International Union of Electricians, the United Auto Workers, the Communication Workers of America, the American Federal of State, County and Municipal workers, and a few others. These unions have come to realize that while there may be dangers in the development of participation programs, these dangers can at least be minimized if there is active union involvement in their initiation. They recognize that some form of workplace participation is coming to be expected by many workers, and they are finding ways of reconciling cooperation with management in instigating such programs while maintaining their traditional adversary role in collective bargaining.

On the alternative side, there is a growing interest in democratic alternatives to the corporate form, featuring a cooperative structure, or various forms of worker ownership via shareholding, which usually lie somewhere in between the corporate system and forms of pure democratic control featuring one person/one vote.

According to a Hart poll, commissioned in 1976 by the People's Bicentennial Commission (later the People's Business Commission), the majority of respondents preferred an employee-owned system to the prevailing system of corporate ownership. Distrust of both Big Business and Big Government remains high in the U.S. While more college graduates are going into business than before, at least some of these are concerned with reconciling the values they have learned through a liberal arts education, and through contact with attitudes derived from the movements of the sixties and seventies, with a career in business. Many of these persons have developed various kinds of New Age or alternative businesses, featuring forms of participation and democratization.

The growing interest in ecology and "soft" technologies has given rise to a corresponding interest in alternative organization forms. Alternatives to the present energy-intensive "hard" technology seem to be naturally congruent with social and organizational alternatives, since both are decentralized and "people oriented." Other trends, such as inflation and a rising cost of living, have encouraged people to turn to cooperatives as a way of achieving lower cost food, housing, and energy.

Partially as a result of the merger movement of recent years, a method of management has arisen that focuses mainly on the bottom line, demanding a high immediate return. When this is not achieved, tax laws are so constructed that it is often in the interest of the conglomerate to shut down a subsidiary and take a tax write-off. As a defensive measure, workers and communities interested in preserving jobs have sought to buy out these enterprises. This has led to a variety of worker-owned, or joint worker- and community-owned firms. A number of these have incorporated democratic management as well.

Often these situations involve threatened or actual plant closings which, when the plant involved is a major source of employment within a community, can have a devastating effect on that community. This phenomenon in turn reflects the increasing mobility of capital, with the consequent ability of management to shift production -- and the jobs that go with production -- to lower wage localities within the United States or increasingly offshore to other countries. This is the almost inevitable result of absentee capital ownership, which characterizes virtually all large companies in the United States today, and is not likely to be changed until workers, rather than investors, achieve not only ownership but also control of the places where they work.

Finally, the example of European successes with co-management, participation programs, and worker ownership -- and the existence of self-management in Yugoslavia and of large systems of industrial cooperatives in Spain, France, and Italy -- has encouraged groups in this country to develop worker-managed alternatives.

## Problems of Creating a Democratic Workplace

If the obstacles to developing participation within conventional firms are significant, the obstacles to developing a system of full workplace democracy are even more serious. Some of these have already been alluded to. In addition, the system of supporting institutions that buttress the corporate system are at best inappropriate, if indeed they do not actually hinder the development of self-managed firms. Thus, the traditional system of venture financing does not work for self-managed firms since it entails control from outside the firm by capital providers. Where the capitalist firm is made up of workers who hire labor, the self-managed firm is made up of workers who hire capital. While favorable court decisions have been handed down in regard to the taxing of worker cooperatives, in many states cooperative law is relatively undeveloped, and cooperatives must adapt the corporate form or some other legal form which has not been set up with the objectives of a cooperative in mind.

Worker-managed enterprises must perform in an economic environment which is unfamiliar with the goals and nature of self-management, and at times has shown itself to be actively hostile to these goals.

The most successful examples of self-management in the West have been ones which have developed a system of mutually supporting enterprises, buttressed with an additional set of supporting institutions, such as special banks, technical schools and colleges, and technical assistance providers. A good example of this is the Spanish cooperative system, Mondragon.

Democratic participation, whether in the context of the corporation or the fully self-managed firm, must also confront the difficulties that derive from internal resistance. Successful participation and self-management requires changes in attitudes and behaviors, and the development of an active rather than a passive orientation toward one's work and its organizational context and goals. The bureaucratic and hierarchic structure of most institutions -- schools, the traditional workplace, even labor unions and voluntary organizations -- discourages the development of an active participatory orientation. In addition to the development of such an orientation, group process and decision-making skills must be developed within the context of a culture which neither encourages nor teaches such skills.

# Chapter 19

# WORKER-MANAGED ENTERPRISES: LEGAL SHELLS, STRUCTURES, AND FINANCING

*C. George Benello*

In the United States, and in varying degrees in most other industrialized market economy countries, legal forms are just beginning to be developed to accommodate worker self-management. (Worker management here means both democratic ownership and control by working members of an enterprise, leaving out a number of other types of initiatives and arrangements similar in spirit, including democratic control of nonprofit organization, quality of working life projects, and autonomous work groups.) Cooperatives and various forms of employee ownership are examined in relation to worker-managed enterprises, as are funding methods and internal structures of worker-managed enterprises.

## The Cooperative Form

Although worker-managed companies share with cooperatives the basic principle of democratic governance, namely, one-worker/one-vote, cooperatives as they have developed have become identified with a set of legal and governing principles which when applied to worker-managed companies create a number of problems examined below. Also, cooperative law varies from state to state, and in some cases is too narrow in its purview to allow for worker management.

Since the worker-managed company has unique structural requirements, it can operate within a number of legal shells -- of the cooperative, corporate, or partnership variety -- but in all cases must modify them through specifications in the charter and by-laws so as to meet its own requirements. A major breakthrough occurred with enactment of a new Mondragon-style industrial cooperative statute in the 1980s in several U.S. states. This development is discussed in the next section of this chapter.

Cooperative law has developed functionally to take account of existing practices. Existing cooperatives are mainly of three types, producer cooperatives, purchasing cooperatives, and consumer cooperatives. The term "producer cooperative" has been used to refer to what we shall call worker cooperative -- the fourth type -- but in fact is generally applied to independent producers joining together to market their product; hence it is better labeled a marketing cooperative. Marketing cooperatives are most often found in the agricultural sector of the economy. Purchasing cooperatives consist of people banding together to obtain the benefits of large purchase orders, and are similar to food distribution cooperatives that involve the pre-ordering and pickup of food supplies in order to obtain the benefits.

The principle of voluntary membership, understandable in non-worker cooperatives, must be significantly modified in the case of worker cooperatives. A worker cooperative is like a mini-republic, with a constitution, administrative, legislative, and judicial functions, and a citizen's rights and responsibilities.[1] Entering members must be willing to accept the laws of the republic as well as be qualified for the position which they seek. Unlike working for a conventional corporation, where the incentives are primarily monetary, a member of a working cooperative must be committed to the cooperative, since the member becomes a part owner and shares in the control of the organization. A commitment mechanism often used is to require an "investment" in the cooperative -- although, as we shall see, it is more like a membership deposit.

The principle of a limited return on capital, which obtains in most non-worker cooperatives, derives from the fact that these cooperatives serve the purposes of the user-members, not investors; they were not developed to make investors rich. In the case of worker cooperatives, this principle alone is not sufficient to guarantee the social purposes of the cooperative. In a worker cooperative, working members invest not only

---

[1] C. George Benello, "Self-Management in the United States: The Movement for Economic Self-Determination and Workers' Rights," *The ALSA Forum* 41, No. 2.

their capital but their labor; both may contribute to an increase in the net worth of the organization, and where this net worth is individualized in terms of share ownership by working members, there can be a strong incentive to either automate or sell out, thus realizing the individual appreciation. In the first case, the logical end result could be conceived as a factory where all previous working members have retired to live off the earnings of a totally automated production process, with perhaps two remaining workers -- a manager and a janitor. The second situation is found in the plywood cooperatives of the West Coast, which are traditional worker cooperatives. These individual shares, originally bought for around $50, have appreciated to $60,000 to $80,000 or more. New workers often do not have the resources of the credit to buy a membership share, so they are hired as non-member employees, thus vitiating the democratic principle of one worker/one vote.

One approach is to treat the collective investment in plant and equipment as a sort of trusteeship, appreciated property held in trust for future generations of workers, hence, incapable of being liquidated. This in turn requires that there be a system wherein the net worth or equity is divided between a collective capital account and internal capital accounts for each member-worker.

It is possible, of course, to forbid legally the sale of the enterprise, but where the net worth of the enterprise would be represented by shares held by working members, the temptation to sell out would always exist as the shares appreciated. A further problem with this system is that new members entering at a time when shares had already appreciated considerably would be forced to put up a large sum to gain membership and hence a job, if shares represented the net worth of the enterprise. Likewise, members retiring or leaving would place the cooperative under the burden of putting up a large sum to buy back the member's share. The Mondragon-style worker cooperative discussed below provides a legal structure for dealing with these problems.

Philosophically, a system in which only part of the surplus or profit is paid out to members via internal accounts, that in turn represent only a portion of the net worth of the enterprise, is justifiable by recognizing that an enterprise represents more than simply the additive sum of the member's individual contributions of labor and capital. It represents a collectivity in which individual membership may change without destruction of the collectivity. Moreover, the collectivity depends on the immediate environment of its community for sustenance, and on the broader environment of the society; the latter dependence, in particular, justified the concept of trusteeship which would prevent the individual members alone deciding to liquidate for profit. The plywood cooperatives of the West Coast have utilized the system where share value is equated with net worth; their history vindicates the theory that this encourages sell-out; they have in a number of cases sold out to conglomerates. They have also, as noted, hired workers who were not members, where the appreciation in share value made it difficult if not impossible for incoming workers to purchase shares. Both actions violate the objectives of maintaining a democratically controlled enterprise which possesses social as well as individual goals.

The key to safeguarding the social goals of a worker cooperative is thus the adherence to a principle of ownership and hence utilization of earnings which is at least partially collective. In Yugoslavia, and in a number of worker-managed enterprises in capitalist countries -- the Scott Bader Commonwealth is an example -- ownership is completely collective. A wage level is set, and the balance of the surplus is collectivized. However, such a system tends to reduce individual incentives, putting a premium on moral as opposed to material incentives. A mixed system, which safeguards the basic collective character of the enterprise while at the same time creating individual incentives, is used by the industrial cooperatives of Mondragon in Northern Spain.[2] As outlined above, this involves separating the surplus into two portions. One is put into a collective account to be used for working capital, reinvestment for growth, and social purposes that can benefit the workers, the workers' families, and the community. The other portion is put into individual member's accounts but is not drawn out. Rather it is left in these accounts and interest is paid on them. These accounts thus represent a second source of capital accumulation for the enterprise and are only liquidated when a member leaves the cooperative.

In the system outlined above, membership shares do not represent book value, and indeed need bear no relationship to earnings. Rather, they serve as a membership certificate, carrying voting and broader participation rights as well as the right to participate in earnings via an internal account. The purchase of a membership share may be pegged at an arbitrary level, sufficient to guarantee a significant stake in the enterprise, but low enough so as not to prevent new members from joining. In the Mondragon system, the membership fee is pegged at roughly $1,000, to be paid in advance, or taken out of the first year's anticipo -- that portion of surplus paid out on a monthly basis and equivalent to wages in a conventional firm. The relationship of the wage differential to the surplus or profit differential paid into the internal accounts is a matter for members to decide, as is the differential itself. Where conventional corporations have a wage differential which sometimes is as high as 1:100, worker-

---

[2]Among the growing number of studies on Mondragon are H. Thomas and C. Logan, *Mondragon: An Economic Analysis* (London: George L. Allen and Unwin, 1982); David Ellerman, *The Socialization of Entrepreneurship: The Empresarial Division of the Caja Labral Popular* (Somerville, Massachusetts: Industrial Cooperative Association, 1982); and Robert Oakeshott, ed., *The Case for Workers' Coops* (London: Routledge & Kegan Paul, 1978). David Ellerman has prepared a Harvard Business School case study on Mondragon, entitled "The Mondragon Cooperative Movement" and a bibliography of English language books and journal articles on Mondragon, both of which are available from the Industrial Cooperative Association, 58 Day Street, Suite 203, Somerville, MA 02144.

managed enterprises almost never exceed a differential of 1:10, and more often are in the neighborhood of 1:3 or even 1:1, the latter being the practice in the plywood cooperatives.

The discussion of worker cooperatives serves as a necessary prelude to an inquiry into appropriate legal structures. The principles governing the structuring of a worker cooperative for optimal effectiveness extend beyond the cooperative principles applied to consumer, purchasing, and marketing cooperatives, although they share with these other forms the principle of "one member/one vote, and hence are clearly differentiated from the corporate form which operates under the principle of one share/one vote. However, as indicated already, a number of modifications must be made to the structure of the traditional cooperative in order to adapt it to the worker cooperative. A number of other legal structures besides that of the cooperative, including a conventional business corporation, can also be used as a shell for a worker-owned and managed business. The choice is determined more by such issues as tax benefits and relevant state law than by the nature of the legal shell in and of itself.

## The Mondragon-Style Worker Cooperative[3]

As mentioned above, a major breakthrough has been occurring during the 1980s in the United States with the adoption in several states of statutes embodying the principles and characteristics of a truly democratic worker-owned and managed business. The first of these was enacted in Massachusetts in 1982 and has been used as a model for similar laws passed subsequently in other states, including Connecticut, Maine, New York, Vermont, and Washington.

Prior to the enactment of this statute -- known as Chapter 157A of the Massachusetts General Laws -- Massachusetts law provided a less than satisfactory basis for creating worker cooperatives. There were no guidelines for a cooperative membership structure in the business corporations statute, while the statute governing general cooperatives was essentially designed for agricultural cooperatives. Neither of these two alternatives expressly authorized the particular capital structure and internal accounting system of the Mondragon model. The best way to realize that model under Massachusetts law prior to the passage of Chapter 157A was to incorporate as a business corporation and then restructure the bylaws in order to transform the corporation into a worker cooperative.

Laws governing the formation of corporations in most American

---

[3]Addendum by the editor. This section is based largely on David Ellerman and Peter Pitegoff, "Democratic Corporation: The New Worker Cooperative Statute in Massachusetts," *New York University Review of Law and Social Change* 11, No. 3 (1982-83): 441-472, which includes the text of the statute.

states reflect the same situation as existed in Massachusetts before the passage of Chapter 157A. Although flexible enough to build a cooperative within a traditional corporate shell, most incorporation statutes provide no guidance for democratic structure. And most statutes governing the creation of cooperatives apply primarily to agriculture coops, as well as to consumer, housing, utility, or credit coops.

The procedure for organizing a worker cooperative under Chapter 157A is quite simple. The cooperative incorporates as a business corporation under the prevailing business corporation law and simultaneously elects to be governed as a worker cooperative under Chapter 157A. An existing business corporation can easily convert itself to a worker cooperative by amending its articles of organization. But whatever the route, the cooperative must incorporate into its articles and by-laws the membership provisions stipulated in Chapter 157A. By the same token, a cooperative may revoke its election under Chapter 157A by amending its articles after a two-thirds vote of its membership.

A crucial difference between a general business corporation and a worker cooperative under Massachusetts law is that the latter must issue a class of voting stock to its members, which are limited to persons employed by the corporation. The statute further provides that membership shares be cast on a one-person/one-vote basis. The Massachusetts statute contains an important compromise. Strictly speaking, the Mondragon model limits voting power to members -- i.e., workers. There is no voting stock other than the membership shares.

Chapter 157A does allow, however, a worker cooperative to issue other classes of stock to members or non-members, a provision adopted to increase flexibility in securing financing for such business corporations and to attract support from the organized bar in Massachusetts. The issuance of such stock must be expressly permitted by the articles of organization, and no stock other than membership shares can be given voting power -- with two significant exceptions. The first is that the articles and by-laws may be amended to authorize the issuance of voting stock other than membership shares but such authorization can be made only by the members, i.e., the workers. The second is that holders of non-voting stock do have a right to vote -- as a class -- on any article or by-law amendment that might significantly affect their rights.

The net effect of these two exceptions is that only if members authorize the issuance of stock other than membership shares are outside investors entitled to vote on corporate matters. And furthermore, a class of membership shares held by the workers will always exist, with those shares possessing veto power over major corporate actions. "Thus, with some flexibility," conclude Ellerman and Pitegoff, "Chapter 157A thereby codifies a fundamental attribute of the worker cooperative: ultimate worker control on the basis of one worker-one vote."[4]

Two other important features of the Massachusetts worker cooperative statute involve "patronage allocations" and internal capital accounts. The allocation of net earnings in accordance with the relative amount of work performed by members is specifically authorized by Chapter 157A. This contrasts, of course, with the typical corporation which allocates net earnings on the basis of relative capital investment -- i.e., number of shares owned. Thus, this "patronage allocation" provision embodies a second critical attribute of the truly democratic worker cooperative -- namely, apportionment of earnings (or losses) to member-workers on the basis of their relative amount of work (ordinarily measured by hours of work or total wages) and not number of shares owned in the corporation (as in a typical ESOP).

This provision has an important tax implication. Typically, corporate earnings are subject to double taxation -- the first time when the corporation pays corporate income tax on its taxable income and the second when individual shareholders pay personal income tax on the dividends they receive from the corporation. Under Subchapter T of the Internal Revenue Code, the worker cooperative may deduct from its corporate taxable income any earnings allocated to members on the basis of work performed. If these earnings are paid to members in the form of cash distributions, they are, of course, a form of personal taxable income to the members. But if they are credited to the member's individual capital accounts, they are not taxable until paid out to the members, thus enabling the cooperative to retain and reinvest, without adverse tax consequences, a portion of the earnings allocated to its members.

But in the view of Ellerman and Pitegoff, the most innovative aspect of Chapter 157A is its authorization of a new type of capital structure known as "internal capital accounts," which (to quote from the statute) "reflect the book value and . . . determine the redemption price of membership shares, capital stock, and written notices of allocation." (The last named cover earnings credited to members in their internal capital accounts but not yet paid out to them, i.e., retained earnings that can be used to reinvest in the cooperative.) This arrangement makes it possible for a worker cooperative to maintain a fixed membership entry fee while allocating increases in the cooperative's net worth to the workers whose labor has contributed to this increase. Thus, the internal accounts, rather than shares of stock, reflect any growth in the equity of the corporation. This avoids the problem already mentioned in the plywood cooperatives in the Pacific Northwest.

In addition to the tax benefits under Subchapter T already mentioned, the Massachusetts statute permits a 157A corporation to use the word "cooperative" in its corporate name. Another incidental benefit is

---

[4]Ibid., p. 455.

the exemption of small worker cooperatives from state registration of securities offerings, which reduces paper work and reporting burdens. The
Massachusetts statute also provides flexibility between a "pure" worker
cooperative structure on the Mondragon model and a hybrid that combines cooperative characteristics with a typical capital structure. This
flexibility makes possible creative financing schemes that involve stock
sales to nonmember investors and facilitates the gradual conversion of
existing business corporations to worker cooperatives. But irrespective of
the mix in capital structure, the corporation must have at a minimum a
separate class of one-worker/one-vote stock held by the workforce.

The Massachusetts statute, and similar ones enacted by other states,
thus represent a fundamental change in the way economic activity is organized and conducted in American society. "Using the shell of American
corporation law," conclude Ellerman and Pitegoff, "it converts the corporation from an enterprise based on property rights to a social institution
based on personal rights."[5]

## Employee Ownership and ESOPS

In addition to the traditional cooperative form and the Mondragon-
style worker cooperative, there is another form, the employee-owned corporation, which in a number of cases has been used to create a system
providing in theory for the possibility of worker management (although
the practice has not lived up to expectations). The employee-owned corporation is simply a conventionally structured corporation with shares
held predominantly by the workers. A number of these have been created
with the help of the Economic Development Agency of the Department
of Commerce. In at least three cases known to this writer -- the
Herkimer Library Bureau Factory, Vermont Asbestos, and South Bend
Lathe -- workers put up money to buy out their factories when they were
about to be closed down, only to find out that share ownership did nothing to change the management practices of these companies. In the case
of Vermont Asbestos, the stock appreciated in value, and as disillusion-
ment with the management set in, the workers sold their shares to an outside buyer after despairing of the possibility of exercising any effective
control; the company then reverted to a conventional ownership structure.

The lesson of employee ownership is clear: when control is vested in
shares and is not a right of working members, this control can easily by
separated from working members. Managers can easily acquire more
shares with their higher salaries, and, just as important, the idea that
workers have a right to control of their workplace does not exist. In all
three cases, workers have gradually come to realize that share ownership

---

[5] Ibid., p. 458.

should have been accompanied by the right of control, but the realization has come too late. The possibility of control had passed from their hands.

In the case of another acquisition which took place after Herkimer, Vermont Asbestos, and South Bend Lathe -- Rath Packing Company in Waterloo, Iowa, formerly owned by Armour Company -- the workers were determined not to repeat the mistakes of these three cases. They insisted on a majority on the board of directors, and were active in developing a system of participative floor management. The 60 percent stock which the workers control is to be voted as a block, thus increasing the possibility of worker control.[6]

Another existing device which can be adapted to worker management is the Employee Stock Ownership Plan. ESOPs (and ESOTs, Employee Stock Ownership Trusts) were created by the Employee Retirement Income Security Act of 1974, an act motivated by a desire to create a "people's capitalism" (following the ideas of Louis Kelso) while also facilitating handsome corporate tax breaks. The act allows a company to contribute to a pension plan via a trust in which company shares are placed. These contributions are deductible from corporate income tax, and thus create a pension plan for workers out of non-taxable funds.

But the benefits to workers of such a system are questionable: the resulting pension plan is totally dependent on the fortunes of the company, and if workers are laid off because of falling business, the pension plan may become worthless too. Also, the stock trust that is created is not necessarily voted by the workers who have contributed to it, but may have an independent board or trustee selected by management or the old owners. In the majority of cases, this is in fact what happens. The net result is that workers are locked into an investment in their company in a way that no externally invested pension plan would do, and they have no voting rights to go along with their investment.

However, here too, a company which wishes to implement worker management may utilize ESOT to obtain the tax breaks involved, and at the same time assure democratic control of the trust by placing it under the control of the working members. As in the case of direct employee ownership, the vehicle of share ownership is a dangerous one to guarantee control. Even where voting rights are made independent of share ownership, and are achieved through the vehicle of a trust voted by a board democratically elected from among working members, with shares voted collectively or as a block, the implication is that control comes as a result of share ownership, not via the more direct route of working membership. As a working member, participation in governance runs the gamut from immediate production and work-floor issues to policy issues regarding the handling of the surplus, reinvestment, new products, and so

---

[6]Daniel Zwerdling, "Workers Turned Owners Find They're Still Just Workers," *Washington Post*, May 11, 1980.

forth. Share ownership, on the other hand, is associated with proportional voting at membership meetings, or of controlling a seat or several
seats on the board of directors, and hence is linked to the present managerial system of control. It is small wonder, therefore, that workers have
been slow to press for the rights of control that at least can accompany
worker-held shares.[7]

In part, the choice of legal shell should be determined by considerations of the desired image. In some cases, cooperatives may incorporate
as non-profit corporations -- this possibility was considered in the case of
a recently constituted newspaper cooperative -- and certain benefits
would accrue to the non-profit status, for example, special mailing privileges. However, a non-profit cannot pay any part of its dividends or profits to members. While this would seem to create an insurmountable
problem for a worker cooperative, certain kinds of businesses -- small-
town newspapers are among them -- do not envisage ever experiencing
any significant level of profits, and what profits that did exist could be
reinvested or used to raise the level of salaries. However, a non-profit
corporation is not perceived as a genuine business, and therefore success
would not be perceived as the business success of democratic management, considered as a system of management. It is also probable that it
would not create the incentives for workers to accumulate a surplus and
to expand, and thus the present feeling is that the non-profit form should
be avoided.

The benefit of the cooperative legal form is that it avoids double taxation; the West Coast plywood cooperatives had some legal troubles with
this when they decided to take their profits in the form of high wages.
But in a state supreme court case, they won their case on the basis that
their high individual productivity justified the high income being treated
as individual wages.[8] For smaller worker cooperatives there are, of
course, other methods for avoiding double taxation, such as the Subchapter S corporation. As we have seen, worker cooperatives incorporated as general business corporations with the cooperative election under
Massachusetts Chapter 157A, and similar statutes in other states are almost certain to avoid double taxation by qualifying under Subchapter T of
the Internal Revenue Code. In the case of housing cooperatives, however, it may well be beneficial to use the legal form of a limited partnership, with the general partner being organized internally as a cooperative,

---

[7]Still, ESOPs can be structured democratically, and there are considerable incentives
for doing so because of the tax breaks involved. See Peter Pitegoff, *The Democratic ESOP*
(Somerville, Massachusetts: Industrial Cooperative Association, 1987).
    [8]*Linton Plywood Association vs. U.S.*, 236 F. Supp.227 (OR1964) and *Puget Sound
Plywood vs. Commissioner of Internal Revenue*, 44 Tax Ct. of U.S. Reports 305 (1965) in
"Draft: A Legal Guide to Workers' Cooperatives" (Cambridge, Massachusetts: Industrial
Cooperative Association, 1979). Also *Linton Plywood Association vs. U.S.*, 410 F.
Supp.1100 (OR1976).

since this provides tax breaks for investors that the cooperative form does not allow, while restricting control to the general partner.

The various types of legal structures discussed above can be summarized in terms of the different ways in which conventional ownership rights are treated. Figure 2 presents five different arrangements.

**Figure 2**

**SUMMARY OF LEGAL STRUCTURES**

*Conventional Capitalist Corporation*

| | |
|---|---|
| Voting Rights, economic profit rights, and net book value rights. | Owned by the shareholders (property rights). |

*Employee-Owned Corporation*

| | |
|---|---|
| Voting rights, economic profit rights, and net book value rights. | Owned by the employee-shareholders (property rights). |

*Traditional Worker Cooperative*

| | |
|---|---|
| Voting rights, economic profit rights, and net book value rights. | Partially treated as personal rights held by workers who own one ownership share (property rights). |

*Yugoslav-Type Self-managed Firm*

| | |
|---|---|
| Voting rights, economic profit rights, and net book value rights. | Membership rights held by the workers (personal rights). |
| Net book value rights. | Social property. |

*Mondragon-Type Social Cooperative*

| | |
|---|---|
| Voting rights and economic profit rights. | Membership rights held by the workers (personal rights). |
| Net book value rights. | Internal capital accounts (property rights). |

*Source:* David Ellerman, "Workers' Cooperatives: The Question of Legal Structure," in Robert Jackall and Henry M. Levin, *Worker Cooperatives in America* (Berkeley: University of California Press, 1984), p. 272.

## Funding Methods

A worker cooperative cannot have recourse to conventional methods of funding involving equity capital that also involves ownership and control. There are ways of obtaining some of the advantages of equity capital, however, without ceding control to investors -- the usual concommitment of equity-type investments.

Equity capital involves two separate components, a variable rate of return dependent on the profitability of the enterprise, and a controlling interest in the enterprise, depending on number of shares held. Both principles are intended as inducements to invest the risk components of the capital, the "front end" funding that is subordinated to all other investments. In practice, however, many investors are willing to forego control via voting rights, especially if they are not majority stockholders, so long as they retain the opportunity to profit from increase in stock price. This poses some problems philosophically with a Mondragon-style worker cooperative, but probably can be accomplished in practice through a hybrid form of corporate structure as is possible under Massachusetts Chapter 157A (e.g., investors holding non-floating, preferred stock, which has prior claim on earnings of the corporation at a higher rate than the worker members' voting shares). Such an arrangement might also be time-limited, thus phasing out the preferred status of the initial investors of risk capital over, say, a ten-year period.

An already existing mechanism through which this separation can be achieved is the limited partnership. Limited partners can obtain the profits from an enterprise, and can achieve significant tax savings through the flow-through of depreciation on fixed equipment and buildings, but have no say in the operation of an enterprise, since this is left with the general partner. At the same time, limited partners have full rights to inspect the books of an enterprise, a right quite consonant with the principles of worker management. Where the tax advantages make such a form attractive, a limited partnership can be and has been used to finance a worker-managed enterprise.

Another possibility for worker cooperatives is for the workers to put up the equity funding -- essentially to invest in their own jobs. In the case where the enterprise is labor, not capital intensive, this may be possible, but such investment should be treated as debt, not equity. In the cooperatives that have been developed by the Industrial Cooperative Association, the Mondragon system of internal accounts has generally been followed. Worker investments are credited to their internal accounts, with interest accruing. In general, it is considered a good idea to make efforts to equalize the debt; in the event that a large amount is owned to one person, that person either develops a disproportionate say in the management of the firm or may feel that his investment deserves other privileges. If the investment is based on share ownership, shares must be made non-transferable, except to a joint trust controlled by the board of the enterprise. However it is done, it is considered best to separate investment and control, with the former being treated as a loan, while control at most is based on a nominal share ownership which is unrelated to investment.

In capitalist systems, the investment emphasis is on control by capital, and a major investor in an enterprise expects to have both a major share in earnings and a major share in control. Where workers are unable to obtain the capital to make their own investment, they are then dependent on various non-standard funding mechanisms for the needed capital. Where the objective of the investor is more protection of his investment than controlling interest, often a compromise can be worked out where a private investor may be given a seat on the board of directors in order to safeguard his investment. Here control remains firmly with the majority of worker-elected directors.

Related is the instance in which Small Business Investment Corporations make equity investments in businesses, which may be worker managed. Usually, SBICs do not require actual board membership from the SBIC, but they do insist on the right to scrutinize operations, and the right to advise in the event the business falters. Since it is possible in any event to distinguish between the internal management of a worker-managed enterprise, which should be free from external interference, and its operations bearing on the external environment -- capital supply, materials supply, marketing, and so on -- an external investor can suggest modifications in its external operations without affecting the nature of its internal democracy -- up to a point.

In countries where there is governmental support for worker management, specially designed funds have been developed to invest in worker-managed enterprises. Peru has an investment fund which yields a variable rate of return, dependent on the performance of firms in the Social Property Sector -- the sector of worker-managed firms -- and which carefully insulates the firm from any possible influence by investors, thus safeguarding their autonomy. In this country, the writer was involved in the development of a community investment fund, consisting actually of several funds with different purposes. Two of them were intended for investment in worker management and were in the form of SBICs. Although the fund never managed to achieve its paid-in capital objectives, the intention was to take a position in worker-managed enterprises as a way of assuring successful growth and also making sure that the enterprise continued to follow democratic principles. Like conventional SBICs, however, this would not entail board membership, nor would the stock of the firm held by the SBIC be transferable.

This is somewhat similar to the Mondragon system, where an investment bank assigns a member of their entrepreneurial division to work closely with a firm that the bank has invested in. The person sits on the board of the firm in an *ex officio* capacity. Just as important, bank sets up its loan conditions -- its investment are loans, not equity -- so as to assure that its entrepreneurial division can supervise the development of the firm. Its concern is both with the business success of the venture and also with its success as a worker cooperative; its 20 years of experience in developing worker cooperatives has led it to conclude that technical assistance is as important as capital. Hence, it requires that all cooperatives it works with accept technical assistance if they apply for capital.

There are a number of cases where worker cooperatives have been the result of transfers from one or more majority stockholders, either working members or external investors, to the workers. It is necessary in considering such transfers to determine what would be adequate compensation to the previous owners and shareholders, in order to develop a system for transfer that ensures adequate incentives. In the case of external shareholders, the transfer may convert the share to debt instruments, with payback rate and interest rates that were mutually acceptable. In the event of an enterprise with little profits, the interest rate is likely to be relatively low, and the payback schedule drawn out. In such a situation, the enterprise will be unlikely to raise further funds until the initial loans are repaid. In the event of good profits, shareholders may ask for a larger repayment or very high interest in order to convert their equity into debt. It may be necessary in either case to replace the original shares with an instrument -- something like preferred stock -- which does not carry voting rights but does maintain a rate of return pegged to the performance of the enterprise.

In the case of majority control held by one or more founders who continue as working members, the situation becomes more complex. Founding members may want to capitalize their initial founding efforts, and obtain a return as founders as well as investors. In that case, if a total sum plus interest rate can be agreed on, this sum would be entered as internal accounts, representing a debt of the enterprise to the founding members. As suggested already, it is advisable to try to equalize the internal accounts of all working members at least up to a certain point, but legally at least, the founding members would then have no more control over the business than any other member. In general, whatever the contribution of a founder to an enterprise, whether as investor, as founder and entrepreneur, or as patent holder, the key in transferring the enterprise to worker management is to devise a scheme whereby the services are capitalized and then converted into debt with agreed upon payback.

The strict following of this system would mean that investors and founding members would not receive a higher percentage of surplus or profits than any other member, since their initial investment of time and money would be considered a loan to be paid back with interest; only as working members would they be entitled to a share in the surplus of the enterprise. This seems more in accordance with the principles of worker management, which places the value of work above that of capital. But a variable rate of return could be paid on both types of investment -- time and money which represent a share in the surplus -- without the basic principle of democratic control being violated. However, if founding members were paid a portion of the surplus proportional to their founding investment of time and money, their internal accounts would grow at a more rapid rate than others; this would increase rather than diminish the inequality between members.

Accelerating the spread of worker cooperatives would be greatly enhanced if a special development bank or some similar source of capital were created. Worker cooperatives cannot, in general, seek conventional equity funding for the reasons indicated above. They cannot seek conventional equity funding, for reasons indicated. On the other hand, banks will not make loans unless there is a subordinated equity position of a certain size. If workers are able to create this position from their own investment, they then have a chance of obtaining debt-type funding from a conventional loan institution such as a bank. But even here, bankers are accustomed to deal with management, and in a number of cases, have refused to extend credit to cooperatives because responsibility rested with the whole group of workers and not simply with the top management. But if workers are unable to make the needed equity investment, then they must rely on special assistance in order to put together a total funding package.[9]

The most effective manner of ensuring the effective use of capital by a worker cooperative is via a contract which protects the right to internal self-government on the part of the cooperative, while at the same time assuring needed technical assistance. The Industrial Cooperative Association has developed such contracts, and they generally include assistance in obtaining capital, technical assistance in developing the business end of the enterprise, and an educational program which will ensure that the members and governing board of the enterprise learn to manage it in an effective and democratic fashion. Since neither the Consumer Cooperative Bank nor the Industrial Cooperative Association take an equity position in the enterprise, but rather provide debt capital, the assistance provided is not guided by motives of profitability to investors. This is important since there can often be a conflict between short-term desires for profitability and return on capital and the long-term needs of the worker-managed enterprise to grow and develop an effective system of democratic governance. This is particularly true since the experience of democratic governance is foreign to most workers and managers and takes time to implement effectively.

---

[9]For concrete suggestions on initiating worker cooperatives, see Frank T. Adams and Gary B. Hansen, *Putting Democracy to Work: A Practical Guide for Starting Worker-Owned Businesses* (Eugene, Oregon: Hulogus'i Press, 1987).

## Internal Structure of the Worker-Managed Enterprise

As suggested, the worker-managed enterprise can be viewed as a mini-republic, with an administrative, judicial, and legal apparatus which defines the rights and responsibilities of working members.[10]    Authority is vested in the whole, but can be delegated to various groups and individuals.  The by-laws and charter of the corporation must deal with membership rights and responsibilities, entry and exit conditions, the treatment and division of the profits and equity, and the governance structure.  To deal with these in the order given, membership eligibility will depend on possession of needed skills, and on willingness to work within a democratic system of governance.  Eligibility will be determined by the board or by a hiring committee, and can involve a probationary period, the payment of a membership fee and acceptance of a membership agreement which spells out rights and duties.  Unlike political participation in the governance of a state, which is voluntary, participation in a worker-managed enterprise is as much a responsibility of membership as is the work itself.  This is so because participation is ongoing and is not limited to the election of governing officials, i.e., management.

Membership rights in a worker-managed corporation are personal rights, not property rights, and therefore are similar to membership rights in unions or other voluntary associations.  Thus, they cannot be transferred or sold, unlike the shares in a conventional corporation.  This can be accomplished by placing restrictions on the membership shares in a worker-managed company so that all shareholders are working members.  When a member leaves, the share will be transferred back to the company.  In such a system, the share functions as a membership fee, separate from the internal capital account in which earnings accumulate.  As to exit conditions, the conditions under which members are expelled should be spelled out in the by-laws.  If a member in good standing withdraws, he will be entitled to the amount in his internal account, although in the Mondragon system, members who leave are given 80 percent of their total earnings -- a sort of tax imposed by the system.

Enough has been said already on the treatment and division of the surplus or profits.  Many cooperatives apportion some share of the surplus to community betterment projects; in addition, a portion is retained for growth as well as the share that is individualized into the internal accounts.  As to the governance structure, this will vary with the size of the enterprise.  With increase in size comes specialization, although less so in worker cooperatives than in conventional corporations.  However, certain functions such as planning, fiscal management, and administration are performed by a specialized management, although often management is

---

[10]Benello, op. cit.

elected from among working members and then given special training. Managers in worker-managed companies are accountable to the membership as a whole; however, in most cases beyond the smallest companies, the policy-making body is an elected board which is responsible for overall enterprise policy, and to which managers are accountable. In addition, most worker cooperatives have meetings of the whole where all members come together to discuss and vote on important policy issues. There are also rights of recall and often veto power that can be exercised by members over board or managerial decisions.

Even in a worker cooperative or other form of democratically controlled enterprise the rights of the minority and of individuals must be protected. This can be achieved by voting systems -- either cumulative voting or a high majority requirement -- so as to assure that minority interests get represented. Also, some form of balance of power and safeguarding of individual rights is important. This can be accomplished by maintaining a union within the worker-managed company, with one of the union functions being to defend a working member when he is accused of some form of malfeasance, and in general to provide a check on actions by the management or board which might discriminate against an individual member. In one sense, a worker-managed company is similar to a closely held corporation where all shareholders are also working members. But, of course, here too unequal shareholding means unequal voting power, and thus majority control may still be vested in one or in a few.[11]

## Education and Evolution

There is no question but that the adoption of a legal structure which is able to deal adequately with the issues discussed above is of great importance and can determine success or failure in worker democracy. It is also clear that we must distinguish between the legal structure, discussed above, and the legal shell, which can be of different sort without affecting the legal structure of the enterprise. Decision as to what legal shell to adopt has little to do with the structure incorporated in the by-laws and articles of incorporation. However, now that enabling law for Mondragon-style worker cooperatives does exist in several states, use of that law does facilitate the creation and recognition of worker cooperatives. In other states, where no such law has yet been enacted, it is fortunate that existing legal shells are flexible enough to be able to embody the

---

[11]For suggestions regarding internal structure and other aspects of a workers' cooperative, see Peter Pitegoff and David Ellerman, *ICA Model By-Laws for a Workers' Cooperative (Version II)* (Somerville, Massachusetts: Industrial Cooperative Association, 1983). The purchase price of $60 includes an hour of consulting time.

most crucial internal structures for a democratic worker cooperative.

Even with the ideal legal shell and the ideal legal structure suited to the size and operations of the enterprise, worker management will not necessarily be effective without an ongoing program of education. Education of two sorts is required: education in the workings of the company to enable working members to make informed policy decisions in meetings of the whole or if elected to the board or to management, and education in group process and decision making as well as in democratic leadership. In both areas, working members become naturally educated as a result of the experience of working in a worker-managed company, assuming they are motivated. In some cases where the motives to change to worker management have been mainly to save jobs, however, workers may not realize the importance of active participation, maintaining the passive mentality that has been bred into them by conventional management. The more working members understand about the overall operations of their company, the better they are able to make informed policy decisions, the more they develop skills in group participation in work and in joint decision making, the more effective they will be. Knowledge and skill are also required to understand what decisions should be delegated, whether to delegate to a group or an individual, and how to organize the production process on the work floor.

The development of effective worker management is an evolutionary process in which the enabling structures must be filled with a content which is learned through the efforts to develop participation. Initially, it may be necessary to rely on strong management, selected for their knowledge of the field and for their capacity to get things done. But as the participative process evolves, the growth in members' skills and knowledge allows them to share more directly in policy decisions which initially will be made mainly by the manager. As working members develop the capacity to self-organize and self-administer, the managerial role becomes more one of general overseeing and planning and of following guidelines laid down by the board and by the membership as a whole. In a number of cases, however, cooperatives have started out with an unrealistic sense of their capabilities and without sufficient understanding of the need for clear job definitions and responsibilities. The tendency is often to rebel against expertise and hierarchy and to deny the validity of both. But hierarchy is legitimate so long as final authority rests not with the top figure in the hierarchy but with the whole. And expertise is necessary and does not prevent democratic management so long as it is not mystified and information needed to make basic policy decisions is disseminated throughout the organization.

# Chapter 20

# OTHER METHODS FOR ENHANCING COMMUNITY SELF-MANAGEMENT

*Shann Turnbull*

## Ownership Transfer Corporation (OTC)

The Ownership Transfer Corporation operates in quite a different manner than ESOPs but has very similar results. It also requires a trustee to hold ownership interests that accumulate with time for the benefit of the directors, managers, and employees. An Employee Share Ownership Trust or a normal employee pension fund would provide a suitable trustee for an OTC, especially if the employees' entitlements to ownership were allocated according to the procedures suggested for ESOPs. These procedures result in directors and employees receiving benefits according to their contribution to the creation of new values. This is a basic condition for maintaining incentive and equity.

The trustee for an OTC would need to hold only one special type of share. The rule of incorporation of an OTC could specify that all ownership rights by shareholders in the corporation would transfer to this one share, at a fixed predetermined rate over the years. The ownership rights of investors in any corporation are quite narrowly defined, and they are

113

limited to five rights: capital, reserves, earnings, dividends, and votes. All other shares issued to investors would lose rights to all five benefits pro rata, according to the number of shares issued. By this device, the ownership of the corporation is transferred without transferring any shareholdings in the usual way.

The corporation could create various other classes of shares and issue new shares from time to time. These would be subject to the rights of the special share. The issue of the special ownership-transfer share, like any other corporation shares, could occur with the agreement of the shareholders without the need to involve governments. The rules of owning wealth through corporations could be determined by the companies themselves. In a like manner, the Trust that holds the special share could determine the entitlements to it that are held or distributed to its beneficiaries.

The ownership of all corporate wealth in an OTC would transfer with time from the outside investors to the directors and employees, who were responsible for the creation of new wealth. Any windfall long-term gains beyond the investors' time horizon could transfer in a similar manner. One reason for employees and professionals remaining relatively poor is that the productive contribution of their work becomes embodied in procreative assets and the corporate organization. Benefits arising in the future from the employees' contribution accrue to the shareholders. These unexpected, incalculable windfall gains provide investment returns far in excess of those required.

However, investors will not want to give up the possibility of such excessive returns for nothing. But a rational profit-maximizing investor would give up all rights to profit after 25 years, so as to obtain a double dividend in only the first year. The extra initial dividend invested at 10 percent per annum would be worth more than all the dividends expected after 25 years. If that investor had the opportunity to earn 20 percent (instead of 10 percent) on money received today, he would need only a 50 percent greater initial dividend to achieve a return worth more than all the dividends he might otherwise receive after just 13 years.

The initial costs of seeking the agreement of investors to limit their rights voluntarily to future profits would be very small indeed. These costs yield virtually unlimited future returns to the regions, states, and/or countries that provide such incentives. National governments could offer incentives by reducing corporate taxes. State governments could reduce land taxes or royalties. City councils and planning authorities commonly provide incentives to encourage prescribed property developments on limited-life leasehold real estate.

A suitable time period for transferring the ownership of corporations (from their investors to their directors and employees or other nominated parties) would be between 20 to 50 years. Higher profit expectation can be provided to the investor by a reduction in corporate taxes or other levies.

The OTC plan is an ideal method for owner-managers of private enterprises to turn, gradually over the years, their operations into cash for their heirs. The advantage of adopting the OTC (without any special cost-saving incentive) is that it should encourage the employees to safeguard and increase the value of the enterprise in the event of the incapacitation or death of an owner-manager. Managers and employees will, with time, become partners with their family and heirs. For the management, the incentive to maximize profits at all times with the OCT plan is that companies adopting the proposal would distribute all their profits each year as dividends. As a result, the dividends received by directors, managers, and employees would increase each year as a percentage of the total dividends paid. Hopefully, the total value of profits, and so dividends paid, would also increase each year and be shared by employees and investors.

The decision to spend or invest corporate dividends (which represent all OTC profits) would become an individual decision of employees and investors. The investors might prefer to place their money in other assets or, if they do reinvest in the same company, to return their money in the form of debt rather than equity. The employees also would have the option of either spending their share of the profits or reinvesting their money in the company (as equity or debt), or investing in other assets. The introduction of these options for the use of profits in modern industrial societies would have profound beneficial effects. For the owner-managers of private enterprise, these new options give new possibilities for estate planning and for establishing a succession of owner-managers for the business.

Because of the additional incentive from the OTC plan for employees, managers, and directors to maximize profits, shareholders of public corporations may also accept the plan (with or without the advantage of tax reductions). Directors and employees could seek the agreement of shareholders to the adoption of the OTC plan by offering various inducements. The size of the additional cash flows that they would need to provide for the investors could be considerably reduced by initiating the ownership transfer ten years after the additional benefits were provided. Directors and employees could then own all the corporation after 38 years, for example. This period would be within the time horizon of management, but beyond that of equity investors. Equity investors in listed corporations rarely have a time horizon beyond five years in their analytical estimates of future profits or share value.

Institutions that plan to hold shares for a longer period may not have any special facility for evaluating long-term future values. They simply may not expect to have the option of selling the shares they hold in a particular company. The OTC plan provides a way for institutional investors, like owner-managers, to liquidate their equity investment with greater profit and less risk than they might otherwise expect. Exactly the same argument applies to investors in foreign countries. The OTC gives dra-

matic economic, social, and political benefits to the host country of foreign investment by providing a method for attracting more foreign assets
and know-how, while at the same time reducing foreign ownership. Advantages such as these could well make the introduction of the OTC plan
mandatory for subsidiary or branch operations of foreign companies.

Because the OTC would provide a way of transferring new wealth to
directors and managers, the community in which the productive workers
reside would also be enriched accordingly. As a result, the *quid pro quo*
required for obtaining the voluntary agreement of investors for the
phaseout of ownership could well be justified by local or state governments. They could provide incentives by reducing or eliminating rates
and taxes, or by providing various services. A three-way agreement might
then be negotiated between investors, employees, and government bodies
for sharing both the income and asset layer of the economic cake. In
some communist countries, such three-way negotiations are made, but
only the income layer is shared. In Hungary, the division of surplus cash
flows from industrial enterprises is negotiated annually between employees, local government bodies, and the central government.

In a private property system, the local and/or central government
bodies could be induced to give investors benefits by the new sources of
cash that corporate management could provide to those bodies. Corporate management could offer the dividends that would accrue to them and
increase each year through an OTC. Strangely enough, because of the
different ways different people value money, everybody could end up with
an advantage.

Investors have time horizons ranging from five to 15 years or so; directors, managers, and workers have greater horizons; and government
authorities have unlimited ones. It may be calculated that (whatever the
total dollar cost of the advantage provided to the investor) any incentive
will be more than paid back by the dividends foregone over a four to five-
year period. Thus, if directors and employees gave up the right to any
dividends they received on the shares that accumulated over the first 10
years to the government, then the government bodies would (in current
dollar terms) gain more than they gave. In the initial two to three years
the government bodies would suffer a cash drain, but they would obtain a
100 percent surplus over the ten-year period. By staggering and averaging
such an arrangement over the many companies in its jurisdiction, the government would always gain 100 percent greater revenues than it lost. All
ownership transfers and all dividends after ten years would be received by
the corporate management and workers, so they would also receive very
considerable advantages. The investor obtains a greater profit sooner
with less risk, so he also receives an advantage. Everyone is better off!

A very vital feature of OTCs, which has profound implications for
corporate capitalism, is that investors would want companies to distribute
all their profits as dividends. The reason for this is that they would lose 2
percent to 4 percent (according to the ownership transfer rate) of any

profits reinvested by the corporation. Indeed, investors could well seek to have the corporation return all its free cash flow. This would include depreciation cash flows (created by tax legislation) that would allow productive assets to be replaced when they wear out. As a result, corporations would have to seek new funds from the capital markets for any growth. If corporations distributed their free cash flow, then they would also need to got to the capital markets to replace any assets that wore out. Thus, corporate growth and/or survival would become dependent upon the enterprise limiting its investments to only those assets that can offer the expectation of a competitive viable return. Capitalistic economies are based on the assumption that such a market discipline exists to allocate corporate cash flows efficiently. But this market discipline does not operate in actual practice in modern corporations.

The growth and/or survival of OTCs would be dependent upon the continued willingness of their shareholders, or the capital markets, to contribute new share capital. However, the value (and so the attractiveness) of new shares would decrease with the fade-out rate over the years. To avoid such a loss in value, a new subsidiary (or associated companies) would need to be set up every two to three years to give an attractive return. In this way, growing enterprises would be formed by a group of corporations in different phases of their ownership transfer periods. The group of companies could have a common management and technology -- like many conventional enterprises that are formed by subsidiaries and associated companies grouped together. Such groups have diverse minority and majority outside interests, and this would also occur with OTCs.

Although no changes in corporate law would be required to introduce OTCs on a voluntary basis, minor legislation amendments might be required for corporations that were subject to a takeover. A problem could occur if legislation allowed the compulsory acquisition of shares that were held by minority shareholders, who opposed a takeover supported by the majority. In such cases, it might be possible for the employees in such a minority to be stripped forcibly of their interest. The minority interest that can be acquired forcibly is usually 10 percent, so this possibility would not represent a problem, after directors and employees had obtained a greater interest. The OTC could coexist, within and between countries. It could operate for wholly owned, partially owned, or listed subsidiary corporations, or affiliates.

## Producer-Consumer Cooperative (PCC)

A PCC is a second-order structure since it is based upon other enterprises. Its purpose is to link together natural resource production and consumer operations in order to achieve the following objectives:

- Avoid excessive returns greater than those required to provide competitive incentive. (The PCC would still provide sufficient incentive for exploiting natural resources.)

- Distribute economic value (created by those with property rights over scarce depletable resources) to the consumers who create the demand, and so the value of the resources.
- Allow communities and nations with depletable resources to exchange their property rights over their fading resources for property rights over regenerative, procreative cash-flow sources that service consumers in other communities or countries.

To achieve these objectives, the structure of the PCC would need to be designed and negotiated for each specific situation. Its structure would vary according to the characteristics of the resources and their consumption. Although PCCs could be established within nations (that include both producers and consumers), they could make an important contribution between such nations since they could be used to eliminate cash transfers. Property rights to the products of resource economies could be exchanged for property rights to the enterprises of consumer economies.

The bartering of a product for rights to future profits in a consumer enterprise would reduce the need for money as either a means of exchange or a store of value. This feature could be especially valuable in the international distribution of resources (for example, oil). Problems of foreign exchange and balance of payments (and of the international money system) would be reduced.

PCCs are based on the production-sharing concept that has been used since time immemorial in agriculture. It is now used more and more frequently by governments of developing nations as a form of "tax" or royalty for the exploitation of their resources (especially oil) by foreign interests. A PCC would differ from this production-sharing concept in two important ways:

- Property rights in the PCC would not be held by the State but by its citizens (directly or indirectly) in negotiable units.
- The PCC's production share would increase with time at a predetermined rate.

A PCC could take an escalating share of production as a royalty, over a 25- to 50-year period, from either conventional corporations or OTCs. This might be done with or without an incentive for the corporation, such as a reduction in the corporate tax. Since a product is obtained instead of cash as a royalty, a PCC in a resource-owning country could market the product locally in order to compete with what is produced by the foreign investors. This tactic occurs in oil-producing countries and provides a means of supplying the domestic market with resources at a low price. Since with a PCC the country's share of production increases with time, the competition for the investor would also increase with time.

A PCC would allow the new value (created in natural resources by their increasing scarcity) to accrue to the citizens of the country. It would capture these new values at an increasing rate over the years. The unearned increments in value that would accrue to the investors without a PCC would become smaller due to a decrease with time in the investors' property rights to production. The primary initial source of a PCC's income would thus be a gradually increasing share of production of its most renewable natural resource paid as a royalty or entitlement in kind. But with limited domestic demand for that product, a PCC might wish to exchange some of its royalties or entitlements for shares in foreign consumer enterprises. The PCC could then obtain regenerative cash flows, even after its domestic resources were expended.

For example, a PCC could greatly benefit a resource-based economy with insignificant demand for internal consumption of its resources (such as a small Middle Eastern oil-producing state). The PCC could contribute income received from its shares in foreign consumer enterprises to a national social security fund, so that the country's finite resources would be converted into a non-finite community dividend. The involvement of a national social security fund in a PCC is desirable in order to distribute the economic benefits of natural resources to all citizens of the community or country with non-renewable resources.

If a nation's resources are exploited by foreign capitalists, the need for both OTCs and PCCs becomes crucial. Only then can a country maximize the economic returns of its natural resources. Without an OTC or some other phaseout arrangement, the resource-based economy does not obtain the best return. Without a PCC, it does not have a secure economic future when its resources become depleted, redundant, or obsolete. The PCC provides a means for a resource exporter to obtain cash flows from consumer enterprises that are based on the exploitation of not only its own resources but also those from other communities or countries.

# Chapter 21

# THE LEXICON OF SOCIAL CAPITALISM

## Shann Turnbull

New concepts require new definitions and may also change the meaning of existing ones. They also involve the reexamination of existing assumptions and, where appropriate, the articulation of new assumptions. The glossary of terms that follows provides a convenient check list.

We think about ourselves and the world in words. To share a common understanding of either ourselves or the society in which we live, we need to share a common understanding of the words which we use to describe our world.

Many alternate models of how the world could work are constructed by scientists. Some are academic exercises; others are intended to represent reality. Often the model or paradigm used to analyze reality is wrong. The belief by Ptolemy that the sun revolved around the Earth was accepted as reality for 1,500 years. Although wrong, this model of reality was still useful for telling the time of day and for navigation.

The natural scientists have now developed words and concepts that allow them to analyze material reality with considerable accuracy. This is not so with the social sciences, which encompass the study of society and its economics, social and political institutions, processes, and values. The reality of social scientists is undergoing rapid change through the development of technology and the global political economy.

The language and concepts used to describe and analyze society in the past may have little current relevancy. As reality changes, so must also the words and concepts used for its description and analysis. In the lexicon of Social Capitalism, new concepts require new words, and these are marked with two asterisks in the glossary that follows. New concepts also change the meaning of existing words, and these are marked with a single asterisk.

Some commonly used words like "capital" are not even mentioned because their meaning has become so ambiguous that the word has become useless for analytical purposes. Capital is used by economists to refer to the accumulated resources used to produce those goods and services represented by the tools, machines, and structures that are described as "capital goods." Capital is used by accountants to describe the risk money or equity subscribed to a corporation or unincorporated venture. The lay person uses the word capital to describe the value of funds he has invested or has available for investment.

The new words and those that are used with a different meaning need not be of any concern to the general reader who is not familiar with the special language and concepts of economists. However, the words with asterisks should indicate the degree of difference between the view of reality presented here and the one used by conventional economists. The viewpoint presented here is based on modern techniques of business investment analysis which use cashflow rather than profit as a basic measure of performance. It is therefore described as the cashflow paradigm to distinguish it from the viewpoint of economic analysis which is based on profit and so is referred to as the profit paradigm. For those with economic training, the difference in viewpoints is outlined in Table 2.

The profit paradigm represented a useful view of reality in the eighteenth century before technology and negotiable assets became influential in the affairs of society. In a similar fashion, the "laws" of motion enunciated by Sir Isaac Newton represented a useful view of reality in the eighteenth century before the very high velocities and atomic dimensions encountered by twentieth-century physicists brought forth Einstein's relativity concepts as a more accurate view of reality. In the physical sciences, a change of paradigms was required because a new area of reality (high velocity) became relevant. In social sciences, the widespread development and use of new forms of technology has changed the economic reality.

The lesson for the non-technical reader is that there are many precedents in history when the most knowledgeable and gifted intellects in the world have been frustrated in the development of their specialty because the words and concepts which they use as their tools of analysis no longer represented the reality under study. In the nineteenth century, scientists developed the concept of the "ether" to explain action at a distance and spent considerable effort to measure the velocity of the Earth through this ether.

## Table 2

## COMPARISON OF PARADIGMS

| Area of Difference | Profit Paradigm | Cashflow Paradigm |
|---|---|---|
| Activities which provide the foundation for economic studies | The production and exchange of goods and services | The production and exchange of goods and services and the transformation and exchange of assets and liabilities |
| Sources of increased activity | Principally labor (human factor) | Principally machines and structures (non-human factor) |
| Source of new economic values | Production | Production, tenure, and consumption |
| Social objectives | Full employment and higher standard of living | Economic independence, personal fulfillment |
| Criteria for resource allocation or motivation | Profit | Cashflow |
| Notion of "capital goods" | Various, imprecise, and confusing, e.g., income-producing assets; "produced means of production"; no distinction between self-financing and non-viable assets | The means by which nature is made to yield her resources more abundantly, evidenced by the means producing a cashflow, the present value of which exceeds zero |
| Real capital formation | Historical savings or consumption foregone | Historical savings or future savings and consumption |
| Basis for economic management | Monetary and fiscal policies | Monetary, fiscal, and tenure policies |
| Concept of wealth | Various and conflicting, e.g., "income," "income-producing ability" | Value of assets less liabilities |
| Criteria of economic development | Increases in per capita income | Increases in per capita leisure, income, wealth, and quality of physical and social environment |

Today the word "ether" and the concept it represented is no longer in use. The same result would occur in economics with the word "capital" if the cashflow paradigm is found to provide a more useful way to analyze reality than the profit paradigm.

At the beginning of this century, natural scientists adopted new paradigms in some areas, while in others they modified or shifted their viewpoint of reality. The same could happen in the social sciences as the century closes. The concepts of Social Capitalism will require changes in many practices and views in management, political science, law, and accounting.

One important change will be the need to replace modern linear hierarchical management structures with feedback circular structures of self-governance in business and community. Management studies will then become integrated with political science studied at the micro level rather than just at the macro level. This in turn will require the development of legal knowledge for designing and linking together autonomous self-governing entities. The law of property will also change if the new rules proposed by the concepts of Social Capitalism are adopted for owning land, housing, community facilities, and productive technology. The changes in the rules for owning assets and in the structure of their management would, in turn, require changes in accounting procedures.

Changes would also be required in banking arrangements, but these would not represent new concepts. Rather they would represent the modernization of past practices. During the last century, many of the words used in banking have changed or lost their meaning. There are also many technical terms in banking, and for reference these are listed in the glossary. The introduction of the concepts of Social Capitalism also provide an opportunity to build different models about the economic behavior of individuals. While these may not require new concepts and words, we need to identify the assumptions made about human behavior in economic analysis.

Ten assumptions used by economists are compared with ten alternative assumptions made by psychologists in Table 3. This illustrates another difference between the cashflow paradigm, which uses the "real person" assumptions, and the profit paradigm, which uses the "economic person" model.

## Table 3

### ECONOMIC BEHAVIOR OF INDIVIDUALS

| *Economic Man* | *Real Person* |
| --- | --- |
| Unlimited appetite | Appetite determined and limited by the necessity of maintaining the organism in a state of dynamic equilibrium |
| Completely informed | Reduces, condenses, summarizes (and thus usually loses) information; in addition, an "imperfect" communication network in the environment also restricts and attenuates the flow of information |
| Consistently orders his preferences with respect to the possible outcomes of any decision | Does not consistently order his preferences (i.e., changes his mind for no apparent reason) |
| Maximizes something (usually subjective expected utility) | Attempts to maintain an optimal level of cognitive and cognitive activity with respect to a large number of widely varying needs |
| Competitive | Sometimes competitive but not always so, or even most of the time |
| Requires a value system only in order to provide a criterion against which to maximize, e.g., profit, utility, prestige, power | Requires a value system in order to provide a framework for the ordering of needs, the selection of information, and the weighing of multiple decision criteria |
| Not explicitly related to the world as an element in an interactive system and remains unchanged as a result of any interaction | Stands in an interactive cybernetic relationship to his or her community and environment, and is changed as a result of any interaction |
| No significant differences exist between individuals | Differences between individuals are significant and important |
| No limits on information processing capacity, so is unaffected by differences in rates of change | Limited information processing-capacity, so prefers slow rates of change, i.e., nearly stable systems |
| Needs are simple and few | Needs are simple and many |

*Source:* Adapted from a table constructed by Alexander J. Wearing, Professor of Psychology at the University of Melbourne, and included in a paper "Economic Growth: Magnificent Obsession," presented to the 44th Australian and New Zealand Association for the Advancement of Science Congress in Perth, Australia, August 1973.

# Glossary of Terms

**acceptor** ▪ one who accepts a bill of exchange as valid by signing the bill. The *acceptor* then becomes responsible for the payment as specified. ▪ one who guarantees payment on a bill, note, or check

**accounting return\*** ▪ See *profit, rate of*

**appointee** ▪ one who is nominated to office

**appointer** ▪ the person(s) who holds the power of appointment

**assets** ▪ claims recognized by society to real or other non-human property that has transferable economic value

**assets, consumption\*\*** ▪ rights to property which represent material manifestations of living standards but do not in themselves contribute to the production of goods and services for exchange

**assets, degenerative\*\*** ▪ assets created for the production of goods and services, but which do not produce sufficient revenues over their operating life to pay for all their costs of creation before payment of taxes ▪ productive assets which do not become procreative (see below) ▪ productive assets which produce deficit values or negative surplus values (below)

**assets, procreative\*\*** ▪ the means by which nature is made to yield its resources more abundantly without an increase in personal exertion ▪ the non-human means for increasing the productivity of labor ▪ assets used in the production of goods and services which have a value in a market economy that exceeds the cost of acquiring, financing, and operating the assets before any taxes are paid ▪ assets which become self financing on a pretax basis from their use in producing goods and services ▪ assets the operations of which produce a pretax D.C.F. (*discounted cashflow* below) index greater than zero

---

\*redefinition of existing concept
\*\*new concept

goods and services ▪ assets the operations of which produce a pretax D.C.F. (*discounted cashflow* below) index greater than zero

**assets, productive** ▪ tools, machines, structure, know-how, and organizations which produce goods and services for exchange

**assets, self-financing\*** ▪ assets which produce sufficient cashflows over their useful operating life to pay for all their acquisition and operating costs, whether or not the cashflows arise from the production and exchange of goods and services and/or from the exchange or transformation of tenure

**assets, total** ▪ value of assets in a business undertaking whether or not they are financed by equity or debt finance. By definition, total assets equal funds employed (below).

**assets, viable** ▪ productive assets which obtain sufficient revenues from the goods or services produced to pay for all their cost on an after tax basis ▪ assets which become self-financing on an after tax basis from the revenues of their output. All viable assets must be procreative, but because of taxation procreative assets need not become viable. All viable assets must be self financing, but not all self-financing assets need be viable if their ability to become self financing depends on receiving revenues from the transfer of an ownership interest in the asset -- i.e., the self-financing cashflows arise from ownership rather than use values. (See *values, use* below; refer also to *values, ownership*.)

**bill of exchange** ▪ a written order by the "drawer" (the one who is to obtain the money from the exchange of goods, services, or loan repayment) to the "drawee" to pay a certain sum on a given date to the drawer or to the "payee." A promissory note, on the other hand, is signed by the drawee (the one who is to pay money). An invoice is only a request for payment on generally accepted terms of trade. A bill of exchange demands payment on a specified date as part of the exchange arrangements.

**block funding** ▪ funds provided for any purpose to be used at the complete discretion of the recipient

**bulk funding** ▪ funds provided to a community for a specific purpose in bulk, rather than being provided directly to individuals so that the community may redistribute the benefits and/or vary methods of delivery

**capitalism, social\*\*** ▪ see *social capitalism*

**cash** ▪ see *money*

**cash contribution** ▪ cash income received in the form of a donation, as distinct from cash received as earnings on existing funds or from sales of goods and services

**cash economy** ▪ the use of money in the production and exchange of goods and services, as distinct from a barter system of goods and services or a social system. The social or tenure (see below) system creates an informal economy, e.g., the household economy of modern societies

**cash leakage** ▪ the expenditure of money external to a community from where it was obtained (analogous to foreign exchange expenditure)

**cash profit** ▪ see *profit, cash*

**cashflow** ▪ flow of money values (see also *discounted cashflow*)

**cashflow paradigm**\*\* ▪ a framework of economic analysis based on cash-flows rather than the framework currently used by economists based on profits. Refer also to *depreciation*; *profit, rate of*; *profit, marginal rate of*.

**check** ▪ a written order to a banker directing him to pay money as stated therein

**C.L.B.**\*\* ▪ Cooperative Land Bank (defined in Chapter 13)

**C.L.T.** ▪ Community Land Trust (defined in Chapter 8)

**Community/Consumer Stock Ownership Plan** ▪ see *C.S.O.P.*

**confluent development**\*\* ▪ see *development, confluent*

**consumption assets**\*\* ▪ see *assets, consumption*

**converse development**\*\* ▪ see *development, converse*

**Cooperative Land Bank**\*\* ▪ see *C.L.B.*

**Cooperative, Producer Consumer** ▪ see *P.C.C.*

**credit** ▪ to trust a person with goods or money ▪ the granting of value or deferred payment

**creditor** ▪ one who obtains money in the future, such as the drawer of a bill of exchange, a lender of money, or vendor of goods and services who is to receive deferred payment

**C.S.O.P.** ▪ Community or Consumer Stock Ownership Plan (defined in Chapter 16)

**currency, hard** ▪ any commodity used as money or as a basis for backing paper money

**currency, reserve and specie** ▪ any commodity used as a basis for money (see also *hand-to-hand money*)

**D.C.F.** ▪ see *discounted cashflow*

**D.C.F. index** ▪ index of the ability for an investment to produce a cash profit, obtained by finding the discount rate which will make the value of all investment cash costs equal to the value of all cash reserves

**debt** ▪ a contractual right to obtain specified economic values at specified times (equity by contrast has no contractually determined value)

**debtor** ▪ one who undertakes to pay money in the future, such as the drawee of a bill of exchange, a borrower of money, or purchaser of goods and services who pays later (on credit)

**deficit values**\*\* ▪ the net costs of degenerative assets over their useful life

**degenerative assets**\*\* ▪ see *assets, degenerative*

**deposit** ▪ something laid up in a place or committed to the charge of a person for safekeeping

**deposit note** ▪ a receipt (I.O.U.) given by the recipient of goods or money, acknowledging that a deposit has been made (see also *promissory* *note*)

**depositor** ▪ one who deposits goods or money for safekeeping

**depreciation\*** ▪ a non-cash cost inputed into the operation of productive assets on an arbitrary basis by the tax authorities and on a subjective basis by accountants, so as to recognize the cost of the asset or the cost of its replacement over the estimated operating life of the asset. The cashflow paradigm eliminates the need for this arbitrary and subjective cost, which is used as the basis for determining profit, rates of profit, and marginal rates of profit -- concepts not used as a basis for analysis in the cashflow paradigm.

**development\*** ▪ increase in the quality of the physical and social environment, as determined by the individuals in the environment being developed

**development, confluent\*\*** ▪ development financed by the higher incomes and consumption created by the development activities

**development, converse\*\*** ▪ development financed by savings obtained from reducing consumption

**development means** ▪ the techniques, know-how, or technology used to produce development

**development process** ▪ the procedures and institutions by which decisions are made on the choice of the means of development

**discount** ▪ a reduction in the nominal price ▪ the price reduction provided to a person who purchases a bill of exchange or I.O.U. before its due date of payment

**discount, percent** ▪ see *percent discount*

**discount rate** ▪ the number of days in a year divided by the days to maturity of a discounted bill multiplied by the percentage discount

**discounted cashflow (D.C.F.)** ▪ the discounting of the value of money to be received in the future, so as to recognize the value lost from not being able to earn interest as could be obtained from money available immediately

**drawee** ▪ one who pays money on a bill of exchange or I.O.U. ▪ a person on whom a bill of exchange is drawn ▪ a purchaser or borrower who draws up a note acknowledging that payment or repayments are due to be paid in the future

**drawer** ▪ one who receives money on a bill of exchange or I.O.U. ▪ a person who draws a bill of exchange or I.O.U.

**duplex/dynamic tenure\*\*** ▪ see *tenure, duplex*; *tenure, dynamic*

**economic growth** ▪ increase of net aggregate of all surplus and deficit values within a community

**economic self-sufficiency** ▪ see *self-sufficiency, economic*

**economy** ▪ refer to *cash economy*; *informal economy*; *political economy*; *two-income economy*

**Employee Stock Ownership Plan/Trust** ▪ see *E.S.O.P.*; *E.S.O.T.*

**endorse** ▪ to sign ones name on a bill, promissory note, or check in order to confirm or assign its value to another as specified

**endorsee** ▪ one to whom a note or bill is endorsed or assigned by endorsement

**endorser** ▪ one who endorses

**equity** ▪ ownership of a real or financial asset

**equity ratio** ▪ the ratio of equity value to the value of total assets expressed as a percentage

**equity, sweat** ▪ assets acquired or created by personal exertion without money (cashflow or barter)

**equity values** ▪ the market value of ownership rights

**E.S.O.P.** ▪ Employee Stock Ownership Plan (defined in Chapter 19)

**E.S.O.T.** ▪ Employee Stock Ownership Trust (defined in Chapter 19)

**expenditure substitution** ▪ the provision of government benefits in a different form of equivalent, aggregate value to the recipients, e.g., "make-work" programs to replace unemployment benefits

**financial self-sufficiency** ▪ see *self-sufficiency, financial*

**fractional banking** ▪ the practice of banks which issue multiple duplicate paper claims to their hand-to-hand money or reserve currency, so that such hand-to-hand money or reserve currency represents only a fraction of the paper claims or money so created by the bank

**funding, block/bulk** ▪ see *block funding; bulk funding*

**funds employed** ▪ total funds employed in an enterprise, irrespective if they are debt or equity funds, and which by definition equals the total assets

**general self-sufficiency** ▪ see *self-sufficiency, general*

**G.S.O.P.** ▪ General Stock Ownership Plan (similar to C.S.O.P. discussed in Chapter 16)

**hand-to-hand money** ▪ specie currency used as hand-to-hand money, or tokens or paper that represent the specie money

**hard currency** ▪ see *currency, hard*

**head lease** ▪ a lease which provides discretion to the holder to give subleases over any part or all of the relevant property

**incentive** ▪ refer to *profit; profit, super; profit, surplus*

**informal economy** ▪ the provision of goods and services primarily for social and psychological benefit of those involved and often involving non-monetized transactions. It is based on cultural conditioning and tenure relationships, such as that of being a wife who does the housework or a political party worker who exchanges services for power. (It is called the "payback system" with Australian Aborigines.)

**investment profit\*\*** ▪ see *profit, investment*

**invoice** ▪ a request for payment by a supplier of goods or services

**I.O.U.** ▪ abbreviation of "I Owe You" (see *promissory note*)

**issuer** ▪ one who creates and sends out a promissory note, bill of exchange, check, deposit note, stock certificate, or like instrument

**Land Bank Cooperative\*\*/Land Trust, Community** ▪ see *C.L.B.; C.L.T.*

**lease, head** ▪ see *head lease*

**leverage** ∎ the use of debt finance to increase the value of assets which can be purchased by a given value of equity

**leverage ratio** ∎ the ratio of debt to equity expressed directly as a multiple of the number of times debt is greater than equity

**liquidity** ∎ the possession of money or financial assets which are either readily negotiable or have an early maturity date

**liquidity risk** ∎ the risk of not being able to provide money when it can be demanded by depositors or lenders

**make-work programs** ∎ programs usually financed with public funds, the primary purpose of which is to provide work rather than to carry on some productive activity or priority task

**management** ∎ see *self-correcting self-management*; *self-management*

**margin** ∎ the ratio expressed as a percentage of the money required to purchase stock and the price payable for the purchase when the difference is financed by a loan or the provision of credit (see also *equity ratio*)

**marginal rate of profit\*** ∎ see *profit, marginal rate of*

**money** ∎ anything that is commonly accepted to carry out the functions of a medium of exchange, unit of account, and store of value (see also *currency, hard*; *currency, reserve and specie*)

**net worth** ∎ total assets less total liabilities ∎ stockholder's funds ∎ see also *equity*

**nominator** ∎ one who has the power to nominate a person for office or election

**nominee** ∎ one who is nominated for some office or election

**O.T.C.\*\*** ∎ Ownership Transfer Corporation, being a corporate entity with dynamic tenure so that the ownership rights of the initial stockholders fade out in favor of others at a predetermined rate with the passage of time (described in Chapter 20)

**paradigm, cashflow\*\*/profit** ∎ see *cashflow paradigm*; *profit paradigm*

**payback period** ∎ the time period in which an investment is expected to pay back all its costs

**payee** ∎ the person to whom a sum of money is owed or is to be paid; the person to whom a bill or check is made payable

**payer** ∎ one who pays

**P.C.C.\*\*** ∎ Producer Consumer Cooperative with dynamic tenure so that the ownership rights of the producers fade out in favor of the consumers over time

**percent discount** ∎ the price deduction as a percentage of the nominal value

**political economy** ∎ a study of economics which includes the analysis of political institutions that determine how the economy operates

**premium** ∎ in an insurance policy, the amount agreed on to be paid at one time or from time to time in consideration of a contract of insurance ∎ a bonus value in excess of a nominal value

**procreative assets\*\*/productive assets** ∎ see *assets, procreative*; *assets,* *productive*

**profit\*** ∎ incentive ∎ an accounting term that cannot be legally defined or determined in practice on an unambiguous basis in most situations, especially with inflation and/or when assets and performance contracts are involved which extend beyond the time period over which the profit is being determined

**profit, cash** ∎ excess of cash received over the cash paid within a given time period (which when measured over the useful life of a procreative asset is referred to as surplus value)

**profit, investment\*\*** ∎ cash profit obtained over the operating life of a real asset or over the period for which a financial asset is held

**profit, marginal rate of\*** ∎ a term popular with economists for basing theories on how businesses operate, resources are allocated, and economic growth produced ∎ a concept not used in the cashflow paradigm

**profit paradigm** ∎ a framework of analysis, generally accepted by economists, which assumes resources are mobilized and allocated according to the profit which they produce

**profit, rate of\*** ∎ an indication of the degree of incentive for investment ∎ an accounting return -- a term not used in the cashflow paradigm ∎ an indicator or estimator of the investment profit

**profit, super\*** ∎ super incentive; super profits need not necessarily create surplus profits, as when they arise before the investment time horizon

**profit, surplus\*\*** ∎ surplus incentive ∎ values in excess of the incentive required to produce an investment ∎ cashflow returns received from an investment after the time horizon used by the investment decision maker to make the investment. Surplus profits may occur without any super or windfall profits. Surplus profits need not be windfall profits, as unlike windfall profits, surplus profits may be expected. While surplus profits may be expected, they are not required to be received to generate the investment; this is their unique characteristic.

**profits, windfall** ∎ the increase in cash profits created by increased demands for exclusive equity claims over assets and unexpected increases in demands for goods and services. Windfall profits need not necessarily create either super profits or surplus profits.

**promissory note** ∎ a signed document containing a written promise to pay a stated sum to a particular person (or to the bearer), either at a specified date or on demand

**property tenure** ∎ refer to *second income*; *tenure*

**ratio** ∎ refer to *equity ratio*; *leverage ratio*; *margin*

**reserve bank** ∎ a bank which holds reserves of the currency in specie and/or distributes hand-to-hand money

**second income\*** ∎ income received from property tenure through rents, royalties, and dividends. While in a two-income economy the second income may be the only income for many, it would represent a second income for those that also obtained income from personal exertion (work).

**self-correcting self-management** ▪ a social organization which changes its structure and operations to perpetuate its functions through its own operations without any changes being specifically imposed through overt means by other organizations outside the organization's own system of management

**self-financing** ▪ the ability of an asset to produce after tax revenues (also royalties, etc.) from its operations or ownership enough to pay for its acquisitions and operating costs

**self-financing assets\*** ▪ see *assets, self-financing*

**self-governance** ▪ see *self-correcting self-management*

**self-management** ▪ the ability of a social organization or institution to manage its operations, but without regard to whether such operations are generally acceptable to society or if they will further the role of the organization

**self-reliance** ▪ the ability of a community to produce its basic food, clothing, shelter, and energy and earn sufficient external income to pay for external goods and services to maintain an acceptable standard and style of living

**self-sufficiency, economic** ▪ the ability of a community to receive sufficient external income to pay for such external goods and services required to maintain its economic standards at an acceptable level

**self-sufficiency, financial** ▪ the ability of a community to obtain sufficient non-government cash so that it can finance such goods, services, and facilities which are required by the community but which are not provided by the public sector

**self-sufficiency, general** ▪ the ability of a community to exist at an acceptable standard of living without any external exchange of goods and services

**social accountability** ▪ accountability of organizations, such as local government and business corporations, to the individuals affected by their operations through providing such stakeholders with the information and power to change the operation, structure, and personnel of the organization. Social accountability is a prerequisite for self-correcting self-management or self-governance.

**social capitalism\*\*** ▪ a decentralized political system of self-governance characterized by the user ownership of housing and community facilities and by democratic local private ownership and control of means of producing goods and services and the credit required to finance such production

**social tenure** ▪ refer to *tenure*

**specie currency** ▪ see *currency, reserve and specie*

**stakeholders** ▪ those categories of persons who have active interest in the performance of an enterprise, such as workers, consumers, suppliers, or community members as a whole

**stock ownership plans** ▪ see *C.S.O.P.*; *E.S.O.P.*; *E.S.O.T.*; *G.S.O.P.*

**subrogation** ▪ the substitution of one party for another as a creditor

**super profit\*\*** ▪ see *profit, super*

**surplus profit\*\*/surplus values\*\*** ▪ see *profit, surplus*; *values, surplus*

**sweat equity** ▪ see *equity, sweat*

**synergy** ▪ combined or correlated action of various agencies which together produce a result that is greater than the results that would be produced by their individual inputs

**tenure\*** ▪ the implicit or explicit rules recognized by society for relating people to institution (social tenure) and people to property (property tenure)

**tenure, duplex\*\*** ▪ a system of tenure where there are two separate but related titles to property. In the C.L.B. concept, one title reflects the value of land and the other the value of specific improvements constructed on the land.

**tenure, dynamic\*\*** ▪ a system of tenure which changes on a continuous predetermined basis with time

**tenure, value\*\*** ▪ economic value available from tenure relationships (for example, see *values, ownership*)

**time horizon\*** ▪ a time in the future after which investment decision makers ignore the value but not the possibility of obtaining cashflows; a future time beyond which no quantifiable economic incentive for making an investment is recognized

**total assets** ▪ see *assets, total*

**two-income economy** ▪ a term used by Louis Kelso to describe an economic system where all citizens have the right to receive property ("second") income directly as property owners, in addition to any income they may receive from their personal exertion

**use values\*\*** ▪ see *values, use*

**utility** ▪ the quality of usefulness or the degree of value to a particular person in a particular situation

**value in excess of incentive\*\*** ▪ see *profit, surplus*

**value risk** ▪ the risk of losing value in an asset, especially assets of contractually determined value, such as loans, bills, I.O.U.s, and deposits

**value, tenure\*\*** ▪ see *tenure value*

**values, deficit\*\*** ▪ see *deficit values*

**values, ownership\*** ▪ values which become available only from the facility of transferring ownership interests in assets. Ownership values can exist without any use values, or they can arise from the existence of use values.

**values, surplus\*\*** ▪ the value of increased productivity as a form of "free lunch" produced without increasing human exertion; the pretax cash surplus produced through the operations of a procreative asset; or the pretax surplus of revenue produced over the operating life of a productive asset after deducting all acquisitions, fixed-interest financing, and operating costs

**values, use\*** ▪ income produced from the use of a consumption, natural, or regenerative asset

**viable assets** ▪ see *assets, viable*

**wealth** ▪ value of assets less liabilities; net worth; net assets; or net economic value of property rights and obligations

**windfall gains** ▪ the realized or unrealized increase in economic value created by increased demands for exclusive equity claims over assets and unexpected increases in demands for goods

**windfall profits** ▪ the realized or unrealized loss in economic value created by decreased demands for exclusive equity claims over assets and unexpected decreases in demand for goods

**wipeouts** ▪ the realized or unrealized loss in economic value created by decreased demands for exclusive equity claims over assets and unexpected decreases in demand for goods ▪ decreases in equity values

**zero sum gains** ▪ a situation in which there is no increase in the total even though the distribution of the units making up that total change

# COMMUNITY
# CURRENCY
# AND
# BANKING

# Chapter 22

# WHAT EVERYONE SHOULD KNOW ABOUT BANKING AND MONEY (ESPECIALLY BANKERS AND ECONOMISTS)

*Shann Turnbull*

Much discussion of money involves a heavy overlay of priestly incantation. Some of this is deliberate. Those who talk of money and teach about it and make their living by it gain prestige, esteem and pecuniary return, as does a doctor or witch doctor, from cultivating the belief that they are in privileged association with the occult -- that they have insights that are nowise available to the ordinary person. Though professionally rewarding and personally profitable, this too is a well-established fraud.

> John Kenneth Galbraith in *Money: Whence It Came and Where It Went* (New York: Penguin Books, 1975)

Banking is just one giant confidence trick. To understand how the financial system works and why it is in danger of collapsing, we must understand the nature of its fraud.

The trick by which commercial banks create money has been of great value in the past. It provided the means to finance the rapid growth of the industrial revolution. However, in the past, the banks that created paper money also undertook to convert such paper into a specified quantity of gold, silver, copper, grain, rice, tobacco, or other commodity widely produced or traded in their community.

Today there is no longer any commitment by the banking system to convert paper money into any unit of production, be it a commodity or a service. As a result, there is no longer any basis for confidence that the banking system is subjected to any checks and balances to maintain either its stability or relevance in organizing society to produce and consume.

Experts now recognize that there is a significant and growing probability that the financial system may collapse. This possibility is also recognized in the financial markets through the margin which interest rates exceed the inflation rate. The margin is now equal to the historical high created 50 years ago during the depths of the Great Depression. Such a high return above the rate at which money is losing its value from inflation can only be explained in terms of the premium required by lenders to accept the risk that the financial system itself may collapse.

Eruptions in the banking system are occurring with increasing frequency and strength. The rumblings among the savings and loan institutions of the U.S. over recent years have resulted in a number of bankruptcies. Bankruptcies of minor banking and other financial institutions in the U.S. have been growing in the last few years. The most recent have also created rumblings in the world's largest banks. The viability of the big banks is also jeopardized by loans to foreign countries -- countries which cannot earn sufficient foreign currency to pay interest, let alone repay principal.

To avoid declaring a country bankrupt, further loans are made to provide the foreign exchange to allow interest payments to be met. In many instances, the new loans are made by multilateral governmental banking agencies, such as the World Bank, or with the support of government guarantees. In this way, the cancer of compounding bad loans is spread throughout the national governments of the world's strongest economies and their banking systems.

While many professional bankers and economists have a general unease about the situation, few are seriously concerned. Even the most intelligent and experienced professionals can be lulled into complacency by the all too human failing of believing that disaster cannot happen to them. In addition, the language, concepts, and institutional arrangements of banking create a comforting facade which generates a warm inner glow of omniscient security. The few pragmatic professionals who can see through the fragility of this facade rationalize that if there is a collapse then their national government will bail them out.

We are thus in a situation where most bankers can observe the lumps in their system but do not wish to believe it is cancer. Those who do see it as a cancer believe that their government has a remedy ready to hand out if the patient shows signs of dying. But here is the sting. They do not. In fact, it is governments that have created the cancer by mutating the concept of money and credit to suit their own self-interest.

What then is money, and how has the concept of money been mutated by governments to create the cancer? Until 300 years ago all money in the Western world was a commodity. The most popular was gold, closely followed by silver with numerous other regional alternatives and/or variants, such as grain, cattle, whiskey, tobacco, and even the North American Indian wampum shells.

Without money, trade would need to be carried out by barter arrangements. Money is thus a convenience to avoid the need to:

- exchange physically commodities or services for all transactions,
- allow the value of one commodity or service to be related to others through a common reference unit, and
- allow the time of executing transactions to be deferred indefinitely.

Money can therefore be described as a more convenient way to:

- exchange goods and services by creating a "medium of exchange,"
- establish a common measure of value or "unit of account," and
- create a "store of value" to allow transactions to be deferred into the future.

Economic textbooks describe money as carrying out the functions of being:

- a unit of account,
- a medium of exchange, and
- a store of value.

Some commodities are more convenient and reliable to carry out the functions of money than others. Heavy and scarce metals such as gold, silver, and copper have proved popular. They can be molded into durable definable shapes which can be used to indicate their weight. Money or economic value was defined in terms of weight of a commodity of a specified quality. Gold, silver, and copper were convenient not only because of their density but because they were also durable and their quality of purity could be simply tested.

The need to test the quality of the various commodities, which were used as money during the seventeenth century, provided an incentive for the formation of banks. The Bank of Amsterdam was formed for this purpose in 1609. It would convert worn and adulterated coins into pure metal and provide the owner with a receipt for the residual value after deducting its costs.

Banks were formed during the seventeenth century in North America to perform the same function. At that time, major discoveries of gold, silver, and copper had not yet been made. The principal source of wealth was from agricultural activities. Massachusetts made the Indian wampum shells legal tender in 1641, and in 1642, Virginia made tobacco legal tender with contracts that called for payment in gold and silver outlawed.

Public warehouses were established to weigh and grade the tobacco and issue certificates to the owners or "depositors," specifying the quality and quantity of the tobacco held. It was, of course, more convenient for people in Virginia to sign over their tobacco deposit notes, and people in Amsterdam to assign their gold deposit notes for paying their debts, then physically delivering the commodity that was accepted in the community as a medium of exchange, unit of account, and store of value.

It was not long before the banks and public warehouses found that it was more convenient for everyone concerned to issue deposit notes which promised to provide the bearer with the specified volume and quality of the commodity accepted as money. Such bearer certificates avoided the need for each owner to sign the note over and so the number of people who could use the notes as money was not limited to the number of signatures which the note could accommodate.

It was for these reasons that paper money was developed independently in both Europe and North America during the eighteenth century. The bearer tobacco certificates of deposit or notes became so widely used and accepted as money that the paper rather than the commodity was made legal tender in Virginia in 1727. The commodity became a reserve currency which did not itself pass from hand to hand like money, but could be delivered on demand if required.

The mutation of the concept of money from a commodity to a paper claim occurred slowly over the eighteenth and nineteenth centuries. During this time, commodity money in the form of gold, silver, and copper was also in use contemporaneously. The ratio of paper money to specie or hard currency in circulation increased through the industrial revolution as individual wealth and the absolute value of financial transactions multiplied. The acceptance of paper rather than the commodity it represented was not only a great convenience but created the opportunity for banks to create money at will.

Again, it started innocuously enough as a profitable convenience for those concerned. A fee would not only be sought by the banker to test and certify the quantity and quality of the commodity on deposit but also for storage costs. The depositors with surplus stocks could recover such costs by lending their commodity/money to others who paid interest.

Again, it was convenient for all concerned not to provide the borrower physically with the commodity or "hard currency," but rather with a note which had a claim to such hard or "reserve" currency. However, a note would have already been issued by the bank to the depositor of the hard currency. Each bar of gold or bale of tobacco would now have two notes in circulation claiming ownership! The volume of paper money created by the reserve currency has now been doubled by a stroke of a pen! To quote John Kenneth Galbraith, "The process by which banks create money is so simple that the mind is repelled. Where something so important is involved a deeper mystery seems only decent."[1]

There was initially no limit to the number of notes that a bank could create. In moderation, such creation of paper money or credit was both useful and prudent as well as profitable. It was useful as it provided working capital to would-be miners and farmers to establish themselves as gold miners and tobacco growers. The loans created by the bank allowed greater production to occur so that the loans could be paid back in specie of the reserve currency, be it gold or tobacco. After the loan had been paid back in specie, the note created could still be in circulation. However, the bank would now be in a position to redeem all its notes into the reserve currency if, in the meanwhile, it had not created further notes/money. In such a situation, the volume of money in circulation could have also decreased in relation to the volume of productions. This would be anti-inflationary.

The unprecedented explosive economic growth of the industrial revolution was financed by the banks, being free to create as much money or credit as there were opportunities to increase the production of goods and services. Unfortunately, this is no longer possible as banks have become overregulated because moderation was not always prevailing. Indeed, neither was honesty. In many cases, one customer's deposit of gold or tobacco would be used to back a note issued to a new borrower without the consent or even knowledge of the depositor. Unless you are a banker, such action is called embezzlement.

But as noted above, deposits of gold, tobacco, or other commodities accepted as a medium of exchange were costly to store and many depositors were pleased to obtain income from lending their excess stocks of such reserve commodities to others. Indeed, such arrangements were more often than not entered into out of motives of survival rather than avarice or greed.

It is common practice, even today in closely knit rural communities and even for city neighbors, to offer physical assistance to each other in times of need without payment. This is especially so in agricultural communities where the hazards of fire, flood, drought, disease, and pests may strike one but not another. In such cases, individual and community survival becomes very much dependent upon sharing and averaging the costs of such disasters throughout the community and over time. Merchant and/or commercial banks developed in the nineteenth century partly

---

[1]John Kenneth Galbraith, *Money: Whence It Came and Where It Went* (New York: Penguin Books, 1975).

from being able to provide an institutional arrangement to formalize neighborly risk sharing in local communities.

The creation of duplicate paper claims to the same quantity of reserve commodity need not even be imprudent. Provided the bank-created credit notes for borrowers were secured by alternative assets or claims, the bank would always be in a position, given sufficient time, to extend full value to all depositors. But quite obviously the bank could not redeem or convert all notes outstanding into the reserve commodity at the same time.

An owner of a deposit note who wished to convert his paper claim to physical delivery of the reserve commodity would need to pay the cost of transport, alternative storage, and suffer the loss of interest unless he made a deposit at another bank. If he changed banks, the first bank could then borrow back in either specie or by a paper claim on the reserve commodity accumulated in the second bank to cover any excessive demand to convert its own paper into the reserve commodity. With such facilities, it became conventional wisdom in the nineteenth century that banks could prudently create paper claims on their physical reserve or "hard currency" of around four to five times greater than they possessed. The practice of a bank only holding a fraction of the "hard" or reserve currency for which it created paper claims became known as "fractional banking." It might also be viewed as duplicity, especially when carried out so excessively as to provoke the failure of the bank.

Many institutions which accepted deposits of commodities used as money never created multiple paper claims for a given unit of the commodity. The volume of money lent never exceeded the volume of money on deposit. Such institutions may aggregate and distribute money, but they do not create paper money through the multiplier mechanism produced by fractional banking. Modern examples of such institutions are the savings and loan associations, credit unions, building societies, and savings banks. Fractional banking with its credit creation is a distinctive characteristic of commercial or trading banks.

During the nineteenth century, banking was organized on a decentralized, competitive, private enterprise basis with minimal government intervention in most countries of the world. The private sector had the power to create money according to the opportunities for increasing wealth from production. By this means, those that created new wealth created new money so that a balance was automatically maintained on a highly decentralized basis. The system worked reasonably well with the value of money remaining reasonably constant over the nineteenth century. There were many bank failures, but as it was a decentralized system, the failure of even large banks did not endanger the whole system.

Failures were created more often than not through note holders demanding conversion of their paper claims to physical delivery of reserve currency. This practice, however, resulted in checks and balances on the creation of excessive and inflationary note issues. Today there is no longer any such discipline. The benefit has been the reduction of bank failures at the cost of general inflation and locking all banks together so that a major failure could cause the whole system to fail. If such a situation occurred, then one would need to go back to basics and create an autonomous community banking and monetary system as was done by the early colonists.

During the current century, further mutations occurred both in the concept of money and the organization of banks. All these changes were created by national governments creating central banks. The seeds of self-destruction in the financial system were sown when the central governments outlawed the use of reserve currencies, such as tobacco, which competed with their own choice of commodity. By this means the definition of legal tender was at once nationalized and centralized. No longer could alternative currencies exist within a country to exert checks and balances on excesses and abuses in what the government defined as money. Governments became involved so as to control the excesses of banks and the frequency of their failures. Creating a monopoly situation in the definition of what can be used as money was a short-sighted solution. There are far more effective but subtler ways for governments to protect the public interest.

Commercial banks could still expand the money supply by creating credits in terms of the government-defined reserve currency, but they could no longer create notes which could be passed from hand to hand as money. The issue of paper money became a monopoly of national governments and their central bankers. However, such notes were convertible on demand by the bearer into the reserve hard currency that governments had defined to be gold in most countries. This provided both domestic and international restraints on the volume of money which governments could create.

Gradually and subtly this one last discipline of the marketplace was dispensed with by national governments from the beginning of the Second World War. In the U.S. case, its citizens were first denied the ability of converting their paper claims to the reserve hard currency (gold), then this prohibition was extended to financial institutions, and finally to foreigners. Many countries, however, undertook to convert their own paper money into U.S. dollars for which foreigners only could still seek conversion into gold. However, in 1971, the U.S. government announced that its own paper money would no longer be convertible to gold. Paper money throughout the world had now lost it one last contact with reality. It had become a sham. That this reality is gradually being recognized as such is evident in the discrepancy between interest rates and inflation rates, i.e., the "real" rate of interest.

We now have a situation where each country has created a monopoly funny money system where money is no longer tied to any commodity or unit of output, or even other nationalized monetary systems, as exchange rates now float. Not surprisingly, the value of money has been sinking, and as there is no longer any chain or even elastic band to tie it to reality, it could well soon become irrelevant and useless. If this happens, as it did in Germany in 1923, Poland in 1981, and Argentina in 1982, people will convert their holdings of monopoly paper funny money into commodities and consumer goods like salt, cigarettes, and even electrical goods to fill the functions of money as a store of value, medium of exchange, and unit of account.

The financing of international trade by barter arrangements was forced upon the modern world by Eastern Bloc countries, which had insufficient claims to foreign money. With the advent of floating exchange rates, it became a general necessity in organizing large-scale exchanges of goods between different countries when a significant time period was involved between ordering the goods and obtaining delivery. The world's biggest banks are now commonly involved in financing such arrangements where payment is defined in units of a product of specified quality.

With the benefit of hindsight a far more effective and efficient financial system could be created by design to replace the one we have now, which evolved from pragmatic pressures of the past having little relevance today. The difficulty of asking our experts in banking and economics to undertake such a task is one of language. Many of the "priestly incantations" used by both experts and lay persons to think about banking and money no longer reflect current realities and so frustrate analysis of current problems.

Quite obviously money today is not what it used to be. It has now become undefinable and therefore unmeasurable. It is difficult to see how such a concept can have for long much relevance or use as the key mechanism for organizing economic activity in society. Hard or physical currency no longer exists, except in the form of coinage, and these have become mere tokens without intrinsic value. Without a hard currency, the words reserve and reserve banking become meaningless. So does the word deposit, except in the sense of the ink on paper that we give to the bank when we credit to our account some value which can no longer be defined either contractually or in terms of physical goods.

So strongly are the now irrelevant technical words and concepts of yesteryear ingrained into the high panjandrums of banking and government that they cannot see the folly of their procedures, let alone perceive how a better banking and currency system could be created. One of the most self-destructive examples is the practice of Third World, and even Second World and industrial nations, borrowing funds to finance development projects which require little or no foreign materials. There is thus little or no need to seek foreign currencies.

Suppose, for example, a country like Australia borrowed U.S. dollars to build a port, railway, and township to exploit a new mineral deposit. It is Australian dollars that are required, not U.S. dollars. The U.S. dollars borrowed would need to be converted into Australian dollars. This would require the Australian government to create more money. They could, of course, do this anyway and so avoid the cost of paying interest to foreigners. This would also avoid spending foreign exchange earnings to pay the interest costs. Instead, governments who have the power to create as much of their own money as they wish feverishly seek out foreign bankers to create foreign money to lend to them at a crippling cost!

As money is nowadays nothing but ink marks on paper or patterns of magnetism in a computer tape, the remittance of money no longer requires the transfer of valuable commodities. When one country borrows money from another, nothing is transferred. All that happens is that a coded telex message is sent from a bank in one country to a bank in another. Quite obviously it would be far more economical for the government in the borrowing country to send the telex message rather than a foreign bank.

However, such masochistic money madness occurs within even the leading industrial countries of the world. Governments pay huge amounts of interest to borrow back money which they are also creating!

The constitutional authority for governments to carry on in such masochistic ways may well not now exist. A court could well rule that the concepts of money, currency, and banking referred to in the constitution had no relevance to what is happening today. This would, however, be a great pity, as it is the concepts of yesteryear to which we need to revert without the constitutional rights of governments to interfere as they are wont to do.

It is, of course, not realistic to expect that governments will give up their authority over money and banking. It may not even be realistic to expect them to initiate constructive changes to create a better system. This is the more likely because a better system would mean a decentralized approach which would reduce the power of the central government's financial *apparatchiks*. To obtain a breakthrough to a better system, we may have to wait for the breakdown of the present.

But while waiting, we could begin to experiment with new approaches, so that when the fragile facade does start to crumble, we have a well-tested fallback position to avoid going back to primitive barter arrangements.

# Chapter 23

# ELEMENTS OF
# AUTONOMOUS
# BANKING

*Shann Turnbull*

A modern community seeking financial autonomy requires four basic types of money institutions: savings banks, commercial banks, credit insurers, and money changers. Savings banks are needed to accumulate unspent income or savings to finance the purchase of goods and services. Commercial banks are necessary to aggregate over time the value of goods and services traded and create the credits and money needed to finance the means of producing more goods and services. Credit insurance is needed to spread through the community the risks and rewards of increasing the wealth of the community through improving the ability of the community to produce more goods and services. And finally, money changers are required to provide consumers with the type of currency required by the producers and allow the producers to find consumers who can obtain the currencies to pay for their output.

As a result of the interventions of governments, the classification of modern financial institutions into these four basic functions has become both blurred and attenuated. Governments have not only nationalized the creation of money and credit but have created a monopoly currency system so there is no longer any need for money changers except between different government currency systems. As the monopolization of money and credit by governments has excluded alternative privately issued currencies with their own interest rate structure, the level of interest rates can now be controlled by the monopolist rather than by market forces. As a result, the relation between interest rates and risks has become blurred and has reduced both the need and the opportunity for credit insurance institutions to exist. The existence of a monopoly currency system also obscures the basic roles and functions of savings and commercial banks.

Before governments monopolized the creation of money in metal or its paper surrogate, money was created by individuals, merchants, and commercial or trading banks. Savings banks, credit unions, savings and loan associations, and longer term depositories of financial surplus, such as life insurance organizations, did not and still do not create money. In various societies around the world, there have been many artifacts other than paper which were used as money. In Fiji, woven mats were used. The integrity of such primitive surrogate forms of money was protected by well-established social relationship and customs. It is useful to remember that money is only a special type of credit and all credits are just a special form of social contract.

Modern savings institutions, which only deal in paper assets, are dependent upon the creation of paper money by either the government and/or commercial banks. The effectiveness of savings institutions is dependent upon the integrity of the paper money. The integrity of paper money is in turn dependent upon either the integrity of the institution or institutions which create it, or the efficiency of competitive forces between money-creating institutions to produce a currency that provides the most satisfactory results for individuals and their savings institutions.

When there is no competition between alternative money-creating institutions, as occurs when a government monopolizes the printing of paper money, the integrity of the currency is dependent solely upon the integrity of the government. The lessons of monetary history clearly indicate that governments cannot be trusted to create sound money.

Even when governments do not create paper money and there are commercial banks creating competitive alternative currencies, conflicts of interest could arise if the money-creating institutions are not separated from institutions who provided a depository for savings. Such conflicts could arise from the commercial bank wishing to create too much money to further its influence, profits, or even solvency. This could reduce the purchasing power of deposits in savings institutions. By keeping the institutions separate, additional market forces are created to exert checks and balances on the printing of too much paper money. To maintain a stable currency, not subject to either inflation or deflation, the volume of money and credit in the community needs to keep in step with the volume of goods and services traded in the community.

There are also operational advantages in keeping savings institutions separate from commercial banks and their money creation. Inflation is created by too much money chasing too few goods: a situation which would be created if commercial banks created money to finance consumption rather than production.  If commercial banks are only used to finance the means of increasing production and the creation of money and credit is also limited for this purpose, then an operational basis is established for keeping the volume of money in balance with the volume of goods and services traded in the community.

While commercial banks may have existed in Roman times and in China from the eleventh century, their modern development in the Western World began in the seventeenth century with the general acceptance of paper money.  The acceptance of paper as money makes possible the creation of new money out of nothing but paper or computer signals -- thus, the practice of fractional banking as discussed in the preceding chapter.

Even with a monopoly government currency system, a basic operating distinction between savings institutions and commercial banks is that the former only lend or invest the funds provided by their owners or depositors, while commercial banks may typically make loans three or four times greater than the funds placed on deposit with them.  This unique feature of commercial banks is the "money multiplier" effect or fractional banking.

Commercial banks simultaneously create both liabilities and assets in their balance sheets by creating non-interest-paying I.O.U.s or bearer notes (money) and issuing them to borrowers who in return create an interest-paying I.O.U. back to the bank in the form of a loan agreement.  For the bank the notes become a liability and the loan agreement an asset.  For the borrower the loan agreement is the liability and the assets are the notes which the borrower can exchange for goods and services.  It is by this means that commercial banks get their notes circulating throughout the community as hand-to-hand money.

While the books of both the bank and the borrower remain balanced, with the value of the new assets created being equal to the new liabilities created, the bank can further increase its assets and so the surplus available to its owners from the interest earned on the loan agreement.  A commercial bank can thus be viewed as an economic vacuum cleaner, sucking in economic surpluses from the community and concentrating them for the benefit of its stockholders.  A savings bank, which neither creates nor issues non-interest-paying notes, must pay interest to its depositors or savers.  The ability of such a savings institution to concentrate wealth is thus very much reduced, whether or not it is owned by its depositors or non-depositor stockholders.

Self-regulation to control both the integrity of commercial banks and the issue of the paper currency which they create can be provided by the force of competition not only between banks but also through different types of currencies created by the banks.  Investors will seek out the currency which best maintains its value over time.  The currencies which lose their value from inflation will be passed over in favor of the more stable alternatives. The stable or sound money will become scarce, to prove the dictum known as Say's Law that "cheap money drives out the good."

The currency based on the output of the most productive technology, and the creation of which is limited to finance the purchase of such technology, will become the most attractive type of money. In a modern society, the value of goods and services produced per person depends more and more on the level of technology used and relatively less on the number of hours worked per person.

Commercial banks can maintain the purchasing power of the currencies they create by keeping the volume of the notes issued in balance with the output of goods and services in the community. Because the currency based on the output of the most productive technology will become the most competitive currency with the greatest purchasing power, there is thus a very intimate relation in modern societies between banking, technology, and the stability of the currency. To create a self-regulating banking and currency system, financial institutions need to be designed which recognize these relationships and allow market forces to provide self-regulating checks and balances.

The integrity of one currency compared with another is revealed by the relative interest rates for deposits between the competing currencies. The currency which is expected to appreciate in value relative to the alternative currencies will have the lowest interest rate. Competition for loans in the lowest interest rate currencies will increase the scarcity value of such currencies and so reinforce the expectation of their increasing in value. On the other hand, the competition for such currencies could tempt the issuing banks to create more money by making more loans. This would reduce their value.

The relative interest rates for deposits between competing currencies is also determined by the money changers. With the national monopoly currencies of the twentieth century, this function is performed by foreign exchange dealers. With commodity-backed currencies, the money-changing function could be undertaken by many different parties, such as the producer, distributor, or consumer of the commodity, bankers, or specialist money-changing intermediaries and market makers between currencies.

The need to convert paper claims into the reserve or specie currency, as and when demanded by the note holders, introduces another very powerful element of self-regulation for an autonomous banking system. Even without indulging in fractional banking, a bank may lose its ability to honor the conversion of its deposit notes into the specie or reserve currency, if it has lost money on the loans backing the deposits and/or if it does not have sufficient specie money in its vaults to match the demand for conversion. These two interrelated consequences can be described respectively as the value risk and the liquidity risk.

A bank loses its liquidity when it cannot deliver hand-to-hand money, be it in specie or tokens, when demanded by depositors. A loss of liquidity need not mean that the bank has lost the value of the deposit. The deposit may be soundly loaned out and earning a good rate of interest. However, if the bank was forced to sell its loan to obtain hand-to-hand money (cash), a loss might be suffered if the purchaser wanted a discounted price.

If the bank did not possess equity and/or reserves greater than the discounts suffered in "liquidating" such loans or other assets, then not all depositors would be able to be repaid back 100 cents for each dollar deposited. This would result in a loss of value for the depositors. But such loss of value could be incurred even without loss of liquidity when the value losses resulted from bad loans rather than from discounting loans.

To sum up, a loss of liquidity may not necessarily lead to a loss of value, but a loss of value greater than the bank's equity and/or reserves will eventually lead to a loss of liquidity. The value risk for depositors decreases as the value of all deposits increases, as a percentage of the bank's equity. This is because losses must first be borne by the bank's equity before any losses are suffered by the depositors. A number of interrelated factors affect the liquidity risk of a bank, but in general, the risk increases as the proportion of cash which is lent out on long-term loans by the bank is increased.

One of the most important functions of a bank is to convert short-term deposits into long-term loans. This practice of borrowing for short-term periods and lending for long-term periods is considered to be unwise for all other businesses. A business which borrows short to invest long can become insolvent (i.e., lose its liquidity) if lenders demand payment of their funds before enough cash has been earned from the investment. Such liquidity risks are very substantially increased in business activities that are also exposed to the risk of losing value in their investments. The ability of a bank to accept such liquidity risks is minimized by its requiring that very secure assets be pledged as collateral substantially greater in value than the loans being made.

The incentive for a bank to accept liquidity risks is that a higher interest rate can generally be obtained on long-term loans in comparison with the interest rate that needs to be given to attract short-term lenders/depositors. Banks cover their operating costs and make profits from the margin between the cost of borrowing funds and the return available from lending at a higher rate. In designing a community banking system, this margin must be sufficient to meet the costs of operation of the bank and provide a return to those who have invested in the bank, whether they be shareholders in a conventional stockholder-owned institution or members of a community-based cooperative who agree not only to make deposits but also subscribe to shares in the bank.

The return on equity increases as the proportion of deposits to equity increases, that is, the more equity is leveraged with deposits. But as noted earlier, the risk of value losses for the depositors increases as the proportion of equity to deposits decreases if there exists a risk of value losses in the bank's loans. Riskless loans, however, yield the lowest interest rates and so reduce the bank's returns. On the other hand, depositors will lose value only if all the shareholders' equity is lost. There is thus a very strong incentive for bankers not to accept too much risk by either accepting too many deposits in relation to their equity or too many loans with high risk value. As a result, there is a strong incentive for self-regulation by banks, which would be at least as great, if not greater, in a community-owned and controlled bank.

Such incentives for self-regulation did not prove to be sufficient in many situations during the era of decentralized banking during the nineteenth century. Additional checks and balances are required which, however, support rather than deny an autonomous decentralized banking structure. The insurance of bank deposits and bank loans provides techniques for introducing such additional checks and balances for self-regulation. They also provide a basis for making banks far more efficient in their function of converting short-term deposits into long-term loans. Efficiency in this "intermediation" function means greater productivity in the use of a community's capital resources.

One way an autonomous decentralized community-controlled bank can deal with the element of risk is by incurring the additional cost of insuring its loans against losses through a separate insurance organization. The ability of such an organization to insure loans at a cost lower than the value of the benefits obtained by a bank arises from loan insurers being organized in quite a different manner from a bank. Loan and risk insurance organizations generally are most efficiently organized by not also accepting liquidity risks associated with having depositors. It is for this reason that insurance companies do not lever their shareholders' equity with any deposits or borrowings. This is exactly opposite to a bank, which seeks to maximize the ratio of deposits to equity to maximize its returns on equity.

A symbiotic relationship can thus be established between banks and insurance organizations, whereby each can be better off by undertaking those functions which it is best set up to do. The banks should undertake only the function of managing liquidity risks arising from converting short-term deposits to long-term loans, passing on their exposure to any value risks to insurance organizations which do not accept any liquidity exposure. The acceptance of both liquidity and value risks in one organization is, alas, commonly done today with contemporary commercial banks. The inefficiencies of this arrangement only survive because of the support provided by the government monopoly monetary system. This system frustrates the emergence of market forces, which would naturally separate liquidity and value risks into different institutions in an autonomous, community-based financial system.

While a bank with high leverage and an insurance organization without leverage can establish a symbiotic financial relationship, there may be many additional advantages for a bank to utilize loan insurance. When the British introduced modern banking to Asia in the nineteenth century, they had the problem of making loans in alien cultures whose languages and customs were not properly comprehended. To manage and accept the additional risks introduced in such circumstances, they appointed local agents to manage loan collections on a commission basis. These agents were known as "compradores." The most effective compradores in Chinese communities were influential members of the local secret society. In this way, the integrity of the loan was integrated into the traditions and social relationships within the local community. As noted earlier, credit is but a special type of social contract.

There are many situations in which loan guarantors could assist in quite constructive ways to minimize the risk of non-payment, especially when the loan is made to finance the means to increase the output of goods and services widely used within the community. The cost of such means should be recovered from the value of goods and services produced, which would then allow any loan to be self-liquidating. Loan guarantors could directly assist in this regard if they were also stakeholders in the enterprise, such as consumers, employees, and suppliers. The involvement of such stakeholders as guarantors also introduces new dimensions of self-regulation for credit creation and management. Stakeholders thus have a vital role to play in the creation of autonomous, community-based financial systems.

# Chapter 24

# CREATING A COMMUNITY CURRENCY

*Shann Turnbull*

Every time we add our own labour to a product or perform a
service we expend energy and increase the overall entropy of
the environment. Every time we exchange money for product
or service, the legal tender we use represents payment for previous energy that we expended. Money, after all, is nothing
more than stored energy credits.

> Jeremy Rifkin in *Entropy: A New World
> View* (New York: Viking Press, 1980)

Money can be anything that people in a community will accept as
carrying on its basic functions, which are to provide a unit of value, a
medium of exchange, and a store of value. Throughout history many different forms of money have been created with a number of forms being
used simultaneously within the same community. Each form has various
advantages and disadvantages that need to be reassessed with modern
technology and in the context of the objective of creating for individual
communities an autonomous banking and monetary system.

Historically, units of value have been defined in terms of the weight
of a given commodity of specified quality. Ideally, the commodity se-

lected as a unit of value should also provide a stable value over time. As scarcity creates value and abundance reduces value, we need to select a commodity, the availability of which remains relatively stable in relation to all the other goods and services traded for money in the community. This requirement is described as the quantity theory of money. Simply stated, this theory says that, other things being equal, prices will vary directly in proportion to the quantity of money in circulation.

Scarce, durable, and dense metals, such as gold, silver, and copper, have been popular choices as hand-to-hand money. The selected metal would represent the currency in specie. When paper claims to such metal were created to become hand-to-hand money, the metal was referred to as the "hard" or "reserve" currency, as it represented the physical commodity into which the paper money could be converted.

If our objective is to create an autonomous community financial system, the commodity chosen needs to be produced by the community. If a community cannot produce the commodity used as its specie or reserve currency, then the stability of its financial system will depend both upon its trading activities with other communities and the relative abundance of the chosen commodity in these communities.

A classic example of how the value of money and thus prices can be changed within a community by external and distant activities is provided by the Spanish conquest of South America in the sixteenth century. The importation of vast amounts of gold and silver from the new lands had the result of decreasing the value of European money by up to five times. This example also illustrates how the stability of a community monetary system might still be affected by outside factors, even if the community could produce the commodity used as a basis for its money system from its own resources.

The inflationary effect caused by an external increase in the availability of the commodity used as a currency can be very much reduced with certain types of commodities in the form of services, a proposition which will be considered later. In the meantime, there are two other important lessons of history worth noting. One is that different communities have used different commodities as money at different times and often there has been more than one type of commodity in the same community at the same time. The other and related lesson is that, in many cases, the commodity used as money has been consumable rather than durable.

Throughout history, gold, silver, copper (and sometimes even iron) competed with each other in the same communities as money. In the United States, during most of the nineteenth century both silver and gold were accepted as specie and/or hard currency for note issues. Congress established the parity value of gold and silver by specifying the weight of each metal required to be worth a dollar. But the market value of commodities changed with their availability. The relative values changed as the availability of both metals changed at different rates. Such a situation required new legislation by Congress to recognize the realities of the marketplace in determining the relative values between the competing currencies.

Congress eventually overcame the problem by eliminating silver as an alternative currency at the turn of the century. An alternative approach would be to do what national governments have done recently. They have allowed the relative value of their currency to float in relation to other currencies as determined by market forces.

Before major discoveries of gold and silver were made in North America during the eighteenth century, a number of other commodities were also used as money. Two interesting things about many of these commodities were that they were locally produced and had relatively limited lives as they were produced for the purpose of consumption. Grain, rice, cattle, whiskey, and tobacco were common examples, tobacco having been discussed in Chapter 22.

The idea that money should have a limited life was put forward during the Great Depression in both Germany and the United States on the assumption that it would force people to spend and so generate economic activity. An advantage of using a consumable commodity as a basis for a currency system is that it could provide a way of controlling the volume of money created and thus inflation.

Commodities which have intrinsic value are those produced only for the purpose of being consumed. The integrity of such intrinsic consumption values is insured by the commodity having a limited life. In agricultural communities, the use of produce such as grain or tobacco as a currency also has appeal because the quantity of currency created will reflect to some greater or lesser extent the volume of economic activity in the community. However, the production of agricultural produce can vary widely and so suffer wide changes in value.

The development of modern commodity markets with paper claims to such produce has created a de facto alternative currency system for those commercially involved as producers or processors. For others trading in the commodity market, the volatility of such commodities is of greater concern as they are exposed to the considerable costs of delivery and storage.

Another option for basing a currency system is provided by services. Generally, these can be produced as they are consumed and so avoid wide changes in value and the cost of storage associated with physical commodities. The most obvious service to consider is human labor. An individual could create a contract note to provide specified hours of a specified service. If these services were deliverable to the bearer of the note, the note could be exchanged (sold) by the creator of the note for other goods and services. This is the essence of the LETSs (Local Exchange and Trading System) which have been established in British Columbia and are emerging in other communities in North America through the efforts of Michael Linton and others.

There is a problem in modern societies with using human labor as a unit of value, however, since the output of goods and services produced by an hour of work depends very largely on the technology employed. To increase productivity, improved and generally more expensive technology will be required. This in turn will require a greater volume of money to finance the purchase of the improved technology. Price stability can be maintained by having a financial system which will automatically create more money to finance improved technology that increases output so as to maintain the ratio of the volume of money to the volume of goods and services.

With much modern technology the volume of output is quite independent of human labor, except that required for repair and maintenance. The automatic elevator is an example of labor in the form of attendants being entirely eliminated. These examples are becoming more and more common as machines replace people and robots replace and repair machines and even run factories. Today there now exists the opportunity for any community in the world to produce electrical energy without any human labor on a continuous basis by the use of wind, solar, hydro, or wave generators.

The production of electrical energy has now become a basic activity for all modern communities. Modern technology, using renewable energy sources, has made the cost of production relatively constant throughout the world. The technology of power production from renewable energy sources are, in general, characterized by diseconomies of scale and thus can be produced on a decentralized basis by discrete communities. For this reason, the unit of electrical power output, the kilowatt-hour (Kwh), has much appeal as a universal unit of value for an autonomous community banking and monetary system.

Money would be created by the owners of power generators. It would be in the form of a voucher or contract note to supply a specified number of Kwhs at a specified time in the future. These notes would be created and issued by the owner of a generator to pay for its purchase and installation. The value of notes which could be issued for redemption in any given time period would be limited by the output of the generator. The notes which had a specified maturity date would represent the "primary" currency. Such currency notes would mainly be held by investors, investment banks, and banks.

Commercial banks would hold the primary currency notes as a reserve currency in like manner to a bank holding gold or a merchant banker holding grain or other commodities. Similarly, the commercial bank would issues its own "secondary" notes, which would be based on the primary notes and which the holder could convert/cash in to the primary notes or reserve currency (to be used to pay his power bills at the time specified). The secondary notes could be denominated in Kwhs but without any specified redemption time. They could be used as hand-to-hand money in the community.

Some of the more important issues to be considered in comparing the suitability of Kwhs or gold as a basis for a monetary system are set forth in Table 4.

## Table 4

### ADVANTAGES OF KWH OR RENEWABLE ENERGY DOLLARS OVER GOLD DOLLARS

| Evaluation | Kwh Dollars | Gold Dollars |
| --- | --- | --- |
| Unit of value | Kwh | Ounces/grams |
| Quality testing | Not required | Density |
| Intrinsic consumable value | 100% | 10% |
| Subjective value | Nil | 90% |
| Changes in consumption | Related to total economic activity | Little relation to economic activity |
| Global activity | Universal | Haphazard |
| Changes in production | Related to consumption | Little relation to consumption |
| Rate of change in production | Relatively stable | Less stable |
| Cost of production | Relatively stable by region and in time | Fluctuates with region and time |
| Cost of storage | Not required | 1% of value per annum |
| Cost of insurance | Not required | 1% of value per annum |
| Cost of distribution | Increases with distance | Changes little with distance |

The renewable energy dollar would be far more democratic than gold dollars, as sun, wind, and/or wave energy is available to all communities in the world, whereas gold is not. It is also very democratic within communities since each individual could own his own renewable electrical energy source to supply his own needs and/or to supply to others.

In the United States, there is now legislation known as PURPA (Public Utility Regulating Practice Act) to compel power utilities to buy and distribute power from individuals or groups who invest in generators to produce power from renewable energy sources. Requiring the existing electric utilities with distribution facilities to pay a "fair" price allows decentralized small producers to sell power on a competitive basis. This legislation provides a mechanism for facilitating the creation of community-based renewable energy dollars.

The total volume of paper primary energy dollars that could be created is directly related to the total installed capacity of electrical generators. The total installed capacity of electrical generators is in turn related to the total activity in the community. The volume of primary currency that could be created has physical limitations which are related to the total volume of goods and services traded for money within the community. No such constraints and relationships exist with a gold-backed currency.

While some communities may have natural advantages over others in their ability to produce cheap electrical power, such differences would neither be as great or as volatile as that with gold or agricultural commodities. The community which produced the cheapest power would have the "hardest" or most valuable dollar in terms of its ability to purchase more goods and services in other communities. While one community could sell its cheaper power to another community, the cost of transmitting energy creates a natural limitation to encourage independent autonomous community production. Gold is not so limiting in this regard because it can be cheaply transported.

The possibility of using electrical energy as a basis for creating money has only emerged in the current century. Over the last decade, this option has been considerably reinforced by advanced technology which permits small renewable power generators to compete with large centralized generators using non-renewable energy sources. Non-renewable power sources are less suitable for defining units of value as a substantial proportion of their costs are fuel and labor the value of which, relative to the original investment cost, may change over the life of the plant. Further technological advances could make small, decentralized, environmentally compatible energy sources even more competitive and so suitable as a universal democratic basis for defining a unit of value.

The new option provided by electrical power generation to create a unit of value and the attractions is offers are not presented with the idea that it should be the only basis for creating community currencies. A number of other options could also be used simultaneously and in competition. Some individual and/or communities may prefer to create and/or use other commodities as a basis for creating a currency.

However, the renewable energy dollar would appear to present a highly competitive option in providing a reference unit of value, whether or not it is also used to carry out the other functions of money in providing a medium of exchange and a store of value. If a community preferred to adopt a currency system based on gold, agricultural commodities, oil, or labor services, then kilowatt-hours of electricity could provide a universal reference unit of value between communities of the world and within communities.

No doubt other reference units of value could emerge with improved technology, as has happened with reference units of weights and measures over the years. However, it is quite possible that the need for an even more universally stable unit of value may decrease with changes in technology for a number of reasons.

Technology which creates a more universally stable unit of value will need to be even more highly decentralized and democratic than technology which converts sunlight, wind, and water energy into electrical power. Such technological improvements will inevitably be relatively marginal since access to sunlight, wind, or water is as universal as the human species. Any improvements and/or cost reductions in converting environmental energy into electrical power will reinforce the autonomy of communities in establishing their own sources of electrical energy. This will in turn strengthen the unit of value in those communities in competition with all other global bases for units of value.

The importance of economic values, and consequently the need for precision in defining units of value, will be likely to decrease as the autonomy of communities increases. As a result, more emphasis will be placed on non-economic social contracts and non-economic considerations associated with the quality of life and the environment. This hypothesis could be formulated as a "law" of value in the following form: The need to define a unit of economic value within a community decreases in proportion to the economic self-sufficiency of the community. As a corollary, it could be stated thus: The need to define a unit of economic value between communities increase in proportion to their economic interdependence. As our current highly centralized economic systems create community dependency, there is at present a strong need to define stable units of economic value.

If we define an autonomous community as a modern nation state, then there are more complex forms of money which can be considered. More complex forms of money can be created by basing a unit of value on a "basket" of commodities and/or services. The basket may well be all the goods and services exported by a country in a given time period to form what is referred to as a trade-weighted value of the national currency relative to other national currencies. This trade-determined basket is used to assess the relevance of the rate at which the national government will convert its currency into the currency of another government. The conversion rate is referred to as the parity value or foreign exchange rate, with the parity rate determined by the government as the official exchange rate.

The value of anything, be it a commodity or a currency, can never be determined by the producer or creator of the commodity or currency, but only by the consumer or user. Thus, if the rest of the world does not require any of the goods and services a country produces, no foreigner will need to purchase its currency and its currency will have no value for foreigners. The nationalized monopoly money created by governments today only has value to foreigners to the extent that foreigners wish to purchase the goods and services produced by the country. No matter what a national government may say, it is foreigners, not the government, who determine the international value of a nation's currency. National governments may declare a rate at which they will exchange foreign currency into their own, but such official rates are still subject to market forces in the longer run.

The basket of goods and services exported by each country differs between countries and changes over time. The basket of goods and services produced and consumed by the whole world changes only over time and then relatively slowly. For this reason, proposals have been put forward to create a unit of value based on a basket of a specified number of commodities, with the proportion of each commodity in the basket being in proportion to the rate at which each commodity is produced and consumed in the world.

Such a unit of value has many attractions. It would be little affected by excesses or shortages of any one particular commodity but would keep fairly closely in step with aggregate economic activity. If it got too far out of step, then the commodities specified to be in the basket and/or their relative amounts could be changed. However, this is also a weakness as it means that there is no reference unit of value which is not subject to administrative discretion as to what commodities are used and in what proportions. Another problem may be the need to provide for physical delivery of the specified commodities to allow market forces to exert checks and balances on the volume of money created by the banking system. With modern commodity markets, arbitrage dealings, and related "paper" markets involving contracts to deliver commodities in the future, these problems could well be minimized.

Indeed, a very well-thought-out proposal for creating a currency based on a basket of commodities was developed in the United States early in the 1970s by Ralph Borsodi. Borsodi based his proposals on work he had done with the world-renowned Yale economist Irving Fisher in the 1930s. A number of elements of this proposal were field tested in the small community of Exeter in New Hampshire for 18 months during 1973 to 1974.

A paper certificate called a "Constant" was created as hand-to-hand money, with the local banks allowing accounts denominated in Constants to be opened. The value of the Constant was based on the market value of a basket of 25 commodities. The commodities and their amounts were listed on each certificate. They included such items as iron, aluminum, coal, oil, wheat, and sugar, with their relative volume reflecting the relative global production/consumption of each community.

The purchasing power of the certificate was based on the value of the specific basket of commodities and so remained constant relative to the average price of these commodities. During the term of the Exeter experiment, the purchasing power of the Constant increased relative to the U.S. dollar as the latter value decreased with the small level of inflation that existed at the time. The vital element missing from the Exeter experiment was the ability to obtain physical delivery of the specified commodities in exchange for surrendering the certificate.

The development of a monetary system based on the Borsodi experiment could provide a highly attractive, non-government-controlled, and competitive alternative to the existing government funny money systems to provide a choice of currencies within a nation. It could thus underpin financial stability by providing a fallback system for the present monopoly systems of national governments. However, because the Borsodi system is dependent upon advanced commodity markets, it may not be practical to set it in place during a collapse of the existing system as commodity markets, in particular, and the economy, in general, could be in turmoil. The Borsodi system may also have less relevance to less well-developed economies and smaller communities seeking a simple, stable, and independent monetary system.

For these reasons, we need to explore further the renewable energy dollar concept and other simple, commodity-based monetary systems, systems which could be used by most communities, on their own initiative, in the event of a collapse of the government monopoly money system. Such systems could well be developed and tested as a community alternative in competition with existing government funny money as was done in the Exeter experiment.

Even in countries where governments jealously and assiduously protect the monopoly status of their bankable currency, there may exist many forms of non-bankable quasi-currency, such as food stamps, green stamps, rent vouchers, store currency, and various sorts of business tokens and vouchers. So development of local alternative currency systems could be quite legal in many forms and permit quasi-banking functions to be established.

The ability to create appropriate banking arrangements is possibly the most important consideration in selecting the basis for defining local autonomous community currency systems. Even in small communities, it may be appropriate to have a number of competitive types of local currencies. While this introduces the need for money changers, there are many precedents to illustrate how such complications can be managed.

There are a number of offsetting benefits in having a number of competitive concurrent currencies in a community. It introduces market forces to provide checks and balances on the competing currencies. People will seek to keep using the currency which has the best purchasing power and try to pass on the currencies which lose their purchasing power over time. In this way, both unsound banking practices and/or currency inflation are inhibited as the less sound currency will be less used. It is for this reason that people stop using government money when it rapidly loses its value, such as the instances mentioned above in Germany, Poland, and Argentina.

There are other more parochial and practical reasons for using more than one currency in a community. This arises from the diverse needs of a community to obtain credit to finance the production of the different goods and services which it is best suited to perform. A currency based on each of the principal goods or services may be required to create the credits to finance their production. By creating paper money backed by the goods or services required by a community, the means for financing the production of such goods and services is also created.

Tobacco-growing areas could create and use tobacco dollars; other areas might create and use wheat, oil, coal, timber, or wool dollars, according to the commodities which are important to the area. Credit notes/money could also be based on manufactured goods or services. It is not uncommon to find bus, railroad, or airline organizations creating promissory notes to deliver travel service in the future for payment today, that is, an advance-payment ticket. If these were made negotiable, they could be used like money. The notes created would provide the finance to produce the goods and services required.

Financing the means of production by such means also keeps the ability of a community to produce in step with its ability to consume and/or export. It also means that it is the private sector rather than the public sector that determines what type and how much of each type of currency is required in the community. This would eliminate the intrinsic inflationary structure of the present arrangement, where it is the government sector that determines the volume of money created. Governments will always find it easier to print money than either to increase taxes or reduce their spending.

Not all products and services will be suitable to provide the basis for a widely used currency. While the natural economic endowment of a community or neighborhood will provide a basic constraint, other constraints are introduced by the need to provide banking facilities. Some commodities and services are better suited than others for banking functions.

# Chapter 25

# BUILDING A COMMUNITY BANKING SYSTEM

*Robert Swann*

Creating a community currency is only part of the task of developing a financial system responsive to community needs. Also important is the creation or restructuring of the institutional arrangements essential to introducing and maintaining a community currency. If we are to begin to design a local banking system which would work for development of the local community or region, what are the elements or characteristics for such a system?

- It would have to be simple to understand, but consistent with our experience of the present system. That is, it would have to consist of both cash (or paper currency) as well as a checking system -- or some other form of bookkeeping which utilized the computer to simplify accounting.
- Unlike our present system, it would have to deal in money that would be redeemable (i.e., exchangeable) in some form in real value, not necessarily gold or silver but real needs of everyday use such as energy. Without a redemption system it will be difficult to convince people of the value of its money. After all, is not

that exactly why the dollar has so devalued -- because it cannot be redeemed for real value by the primary issuer (i.e., the U.S. Government)?

- Most important, we would need to establish a measurement of value that would be as universal as possible and not subject to swings in value up or down as obtains in our present money system. In other words, it would have to remain as constant in value as possible in order to establish a sense of permanency and security as well as make it more practical for exchange to take place. Such a method of measurement would be the most revolutionary element in the design and would be the key factor in making possible a universal system of money and banking, *without the need of central banks or central governments becoming involved in money issues*. Once this standard of value has been arrived at, it could be monitored by the state or federal government just as the Bureau of Standards maintains and monitors other standards of measurement, such as weights and units of space. But it would not require state intervention into the economic sphere as is now the case.

- And finally, a community banking system would have to be organized at the local level and controlled by the community as a whole (i.e., each community would elect members of the board of the issuing bank, which would preferably be a non-profit institution). Under such a structure, banking would become more truly a profession, and bankers would be paid for their services, but the community would decide how and where its savings are to be invested.

In order to make as clear as possible what is suggested here, I would like to make a simple proposal that we consider using some form of energy as the unit of measurement and as the reserve currency for redemption purposes. The so-called energy crisis has made it clear to almost everyone that energy is the key factor in all forms of production and in meeting the needs of society as a whole. In this respect, gold, as the traditional form of reserve currency, is being replaced by commodities or resources which provide essential energy. Thus, oil is referred to as "black gold."

In brief, to outline how this could take place, let us begin with energy production. Almost every community has renewable resources for producing energy. Such resources could be wood, wind, hydro, or waste material which can be burned in a modern furnace such as a pyrolytic burner which converts wood wastes or other wastes into gas, oil, or charcoal. All such energy sources can be converted into electricity or measured in kilowatt-hours.

First, then, would be the creation of a community-based organization, possibly set up as a cooperative, as a worker-owned business, or owned by a Community Development Corporation, to produce energy from any or all of the locally available sources. This organization would offer for sale notes, called energy notes, at the going rate of electricity. For example, if local utility rates are presently 10 cents a kilowatt-hour, then one dollar would buy 10 kilowatt-hours for future delivery. Owners of the notes, sold in lots of 10, 50, and 100 units (comparable to current values of one, five, and ten dollars), would hold these notes for future redemption in kilowatts -- no matter what their future dollar rate. In effect, these owners would have a guarantee against future inflation of electric rates. This would be the attraction for purchase of notes. The community organization or corporation would issue the notes only in amounts equal to their projected output of electricity, thus avoiding inflation of the currency.

The organization/corporation would then invest the dollars received in exchange for the energy notes for equipment to produce energy locally. This equipment could be pyrolytic converters for wood waste, wind generators for a "wind park," or generators for hydroelectric, depending upon the most abundant source of renewable energy available in any particular location. Up-to-date cost analysis demonstrates that such intermediate technology can compete favorably with oil, coal, and nuclear technology in today's markets -- assuming proper conditions (such as tested wind sites) exist.

For example, a wind park capable of producing 1.25 megawatts of power could be established for a capital investment of less than $2 million, using 25 machines each averaging 170,000 kilowatt-hours per year. Assuming an average family needs around 5,000 kilowatt-hours a year, the production of the wind park would be sufficient for 800 families. Current costs of nuclear power for new installations are running several times the capital investment to produce the equivalent amount of electricity.

The electricity generated would be fed directly onto the existing grids of utility companies under the PURPA legislation mentioned in the last chapter. The utility company would either pay cash for the electricity so generated or, ideally, would agree to accept the energy notes issued by the energy cooperative or similar community-based corporation, in payment for bills of its customers, kilowatt-hour for kilowatt-hour. Such a system would constitute the best way of redeeming the energy notes. For instance, assume Mary Smith has bought 5,000 kilowatt-hours for $500. That would mean that at any time in the future, Mary could pay an electric bill of 500 kilowatt-hours with five of her 50 100-kilowatt-hour notes.

The utility company would have to agree to accept such payments in advance of selling energy notes. Some utilities may be willing to do so and others not. However, if there were a broad base of pubic support for the concept, including environmental, anti-nuclear, and other citizen groups, it would be difficult for utilities to refuse a reasonable proposal. PURPA legislation requires utilities to accept or buy such energy, but does not specify the terms of the sale. These terms are left up to state-regulated public power commissions. In either case, under the same PURPA legislation, the utility companies are required to carry independently produced electricity on their grid.

The validity of the energy notes does not, however, rest on the agreement of the utility companies to redeem the notes. The community corporation that originally issued the notes might ultimately be the redeemer based on its cash income which would increase as electric rates increase. The investor in energy notes could still receive 10 kilowatt-hours of value in the future for a 10-kilowatt-hour energy note purchase today.

Redemption is one concern for the creation of an appropriate currency; liquidity is another. Assume that John Jones purchased energy notes equal to 10,000 kilowatt-hours of electricity. Knowing that as a single man he only consumes about 3,000 kilowatt-hours of electricity per year, he has made an investment in his future as well as an investment in his community's self-reliance. But unexpectedly, John finds he needs cash today. He might sell the energy notes to a friend, or barter them for services he needs. However, if a bank would accept the notes, it would provide Stanley with a broader base for the sale of his energy futures. It is the appropriate function of banks to be the managers of money -- to deal with the question of liquidity. A local bank has an important function in the creation of a community-based currency.

A local bank could buy and trade in energy notes like it might foreign currency or securities. The dollar value of the energy notes would fluctuate as the price of electricity increased. Another institution might be set up to provide the same function, but a bank already has the staff and processing equipment to handle the management of money. Such equipment and staff would be costly to duplicate.

In order for a local bank to agree to accept energy notes, it would have to have confidence in the capability of the community corporation initiating the project. But again, broad-based public support would make it hard for the bank to resist handling the new currency. Soon other companies besides the utility company might accept energy notes in payment for bills. Mary Smith might open a savings account with her extra energy notes. Before long, there could be a broad local market and trade in energy notes -- all traded with the confidence that ultimately this currency, at least, is redeemable for something of real value -- energy that can heat the home or warm the meal or produce the light to read by. All with the added satisfaction that this energy was produced locally from renewable resources.

Actually, what has then been outlined above is a way for communities to finance the production of their own energy by the issuing of energy notes. The community development movement is badly in need of capital. This "self-financing principle" once grasped is a very useful and flexible tool for community development.

Still, the question remains of how to capture the value gained in this trade of energy notes and retain it within the community. It is a question of community reinvestment. Although banks are the proper managers of money -- essentially dealing with accounting questions -- they are not necessarily the most competent to make decisions about the lending of money. As to the question of lending community capital, an ethical dimension should be at work. Social and ecological considerations should come into play as well as purely short-term financial considerations.

But how is this not-for-profit dimension brought into banking? Credit unions come the closest to a community group establishing its own criteria for lending. However, credit union legislation and the high cost of overhead limit the scope and flexibility of credit unions. Working with a local bank, which has facility and staff already in place and experience in the managing of money, would make good sense. An interested community group could open a separate account in the bank, designating that deposits to that account be loaned only for specific purposes, such as providing increased community self-reliance in the areas of food, energy, housing, and essential services. The depositors would assume all the risk. However, with demonstrated community support for the businesses receiving the loans, the chances for the success of those businesses would be very good. Although the interest rate to the depositor might initially be lower than available from money markets, in the long run, the return would be higher in terms of local availability of basic items. Such a fund could begin with U.S. dollars, then gradually accept deposits of energy notes. A percentage of each loan could be made in the new currency, facilitating and expanding its circulation.

In any case, a community-based fund has merit even without the energy notes. Small local banks are looking for innovative ideas to draw in depositors and depositors, are increasingly seeking ecologically and social responsible investment opportunities. A community development fund along these lines known as SHARE (Self-Help Association for a Regional Economy), in which a local bank is administering the accounts of the members, has already been established in the Berkshire region in Western Massachusetts (see Chapter 3).

The Continental Savings and Loan Association of San Francisco has been running a Safe Energy Fund since 1979 with good results. Initiated by the Solar Center (432 28th Street, San Francisco, CA 94131), it accepts deposits in the fund, paying current money market rates to depositors, and then using the money only for solar loans in the San Francisco area.

The unsettled times mandate that we consider the options that are open to local community groups, working together to establish economic systems on a human scale in harmony with wise use of land and natural resources.

# Chapter 26

# COMMUNITY FINANCING AND RESOURCE OPTIMIZATION

*C. George Benello*

Community-based currencies and related approaches to local economic change not only offer the prospect of increasing the quality of life and achieving a more equitable distribution of opportunity within the community. They also can lead to a more efficient utilization of human and natural resources in the community. Orthodox economic analysis assumes a relatively fixed set of costs involved in the operation of a local economy. Thus, a local economy has only a very limited set of responses in the face of deteriorating macroeconomic conditions. As the private sector deteriorates, so will the public sector. Institutional and public/private sector barriers are presumed to be unyielding from this perspective. It is also assumed that both the nature and the degree of dependency on the external macroeconomy is unchanging.

This analysis starts off from a different perspective. It considers the totality of resources available to the community by category both within the public and the private sector, and then considers what changes, technological, legal, and organizational, could be made so as to optimize the use of these resources and hence improve the quality of life within the community.

The appropriate unit for such an analysis of a community is probably the county, as human services are often coordinated at this level. In many communities, it also involves a planning unit concerned with mixed urban and rural land use capable of creating a greater degree of self-sufficiency than a planning program limited to an urban economy would be. The approach suggested works best in small- to medium-sized communities of 20,000 to 100,000. But some of the solutions it points to have historically been used in cities as well as in smaller communities.

Two assumptions govern the approach suggested here. The first is that the concentration of economic and political power is excessive and has destructive consequences; local communities are largely devoid of significant economic or political control over their own functioning. Second, countering this trend toward concentration of power can create not only empowerment but efficiency. In other words, decentralization in many cases reduces costs.

There are a number of theories of community and regional economic development, such as central place theories, export-based models, and input-output theory. However, none of these models are sufficiently comprehensive given the objective of systematically optimizing the use of a community's human and natural resources. This is true for two reasons. First, to optimize resources, not only the quantity but the character of a community's internal economic transactions must be changed. Steps to eliminate external dependencies must be taken, which as we shall see require institutional changes. Second, a number of new institutions can contribute significantly to both reducing external dependence and optimizing the character of internal transactions.

The approach that starts with resource usage, allocation, derivation, and resource flows has the advantage in that it establishes a comprehensive development plan, based on objectives likely to be very broadly acceptable within the community and thus not subject to criticism as either special interest pleading or as ideologically motivated. Also, the effort to optimize the community's resources conjoins structural and institutional concerns with material concerns, involving changed and more appropriate technologies, methods of using idle resources, and the identification of destructive forms of external dependency.

Thus, the effort can appeal to a broad and varied set of community interests, involving people with varied sets of skills. It can become an effective mobilizing strategy capable of eliciting widespread community support around a recognition of the need to eliminate blockages and inefficiencies, deriving from existing internal institutional arrangements as well as from destructive forms of external dependency. In other words, the approach will be educative, creating a context in which significant alternatives can be broached and considered.

Some of the approaches that need to and can be implemented involve the elimination of blockages or the reorganization of existing institutions. If low-cost housing is considered important, changes in building codes may be desirable so as to allow for owner improvements or sweat equity, simpler building methods, cheaper materials, and so forth. Or a garbage collection cooperative can be created through reallocating funds for municipal services (as in San Francisco); alternative schooling via tuition vouchers can be developed; access to low-cost energy and energy equipment can be implemented via an energy cooperative. The examples indicate the approach to costs suggested: education alternatives are obviously important since 60 to 70 percent of the budget in small towns is devoted to education. But the other suggested projects lie on the borderline between the public and private sector or involve both. The general approach suggested here involves voluntarism, aided by initiatives coming from local government.

Even a cursory look at the existing resources of a community will demonstrate, especially now, that significant changes in the direction of greater self-sufficiency and more effective use of existing resources requires capital investment. More than the elimination of blockages is necessary. For the human resources of the community to be used optimally for their own benefit and for the benefit of the community, capitalization for jobs is necessary. Many cost-effective projects -- a local hydro utility, street cars or dial-a-buses, solarization of public buildings -- are dependent on external markets for capital, and when capital is scarce, these projects can only be financed at a high cost.

Capital availability is nationally -- or internationally -- determined. This truism underscores the extent to which corporate concentration of power, a centralized banking system, and centralized government economic policy create forms of dependency which make communities (and even states, as Lee Webb's Vermont study indicates) mirror Third World dependencies on First World countries. Exceptions to this exist within the informal economy, where barter is prevalent outside of the mainstream market economy, but while recent studies have established the large size of the informal economy, its ability to attract capital is minimal.[1] Multi-million-dollar corporate barter systems also exist, enabling corporations to avoid cash transactions and often taxes and deferred payment involving interest as well.

Interest rates are set nationally by the banking system and are a function of inflation, a product of government borrowing, the ability of concentrated corporate oligopolies to control markets, and subsequently determined wage-price spirals. The actual cost of servicing a loan is perhaps .5 to 3 percent, depending, of course, on its size. Interest rates in-

---

[1]Several major works on the informal economy have appeared recently, including Graeme Shankland, *Wonted Work: A Guide to the Informal Economy* (New York: The Bootstrap Press, 1988); William M. Nicholls and William A. Dyson, *The Informal Economy -- Where People Are the Bottom Line* (Ottawa: The Vanier Institute of the Family, 1983); and David P. Ross and Peter J. Usher, *From the Roots Up: Economic Development as if Community Mattered* (New York: The Bootstrap Press, 1986).

clude this cost, plus the cost of inflation, which they must reflect. Heavy government borrowing may well push up interest rates beyond the inflation rate. Both interest and inflation rates represent taxes levied on the public as a result of the exercise of concentrated forms of private and public power. Local communities, however, are potentially independent of these national phenomena, although they suffer from local, and largely controllable, forms of inflation.

Historically, in times of hyperinflation or capital shortages, communities in North America and elsewhere have resorted to various devices to avoid their destructive impact. During the Great Depression, cities printed their own currency or tried other strategies to cope with the crisis. This works to the extent that a community is able to maintain a viable internal economy which provides the necessities of life independent of transactions with the outside.

In post-World War II Japan, there were essentially two currencies: the official yen currency and a secondary currency of promissory notes. Unlike ordinary credit, which is non-transferable, promissory notes could be signed over to another creditor and this process would continue for the life of the note, which was usually of several months' duration. These notes, circulating with the endorsement of each subsequent user, represented a short-term secondary currency, based on the promise to pay in the primary currency. Thus, they added to the money supply at a time of capital shortage, although admittedly they were subject to going interest rates, and may, like the present credit card economy, have added to inflation.

For interest rates to be autonomously determined, a local currency must be able to circulate sufficiently so that a significant portion of all wages could be paid in the local currency. Wage earners would then be able to make purchases without exchanging dollars for local currency and therefore avoid dollar inflation. Thus, to the extent that the local currency system was autonomous, it could then be used as a source of credit for low-interest house mortgages, although not for car loans, since whatever the dealer accepted, the cars would ultimately have to be paid for in dollars.

This brings us to another condition needed in order to create a local currency system that is independent of national economic forces and hence subject only to local inflationary factors, and that also is able to avoid high interest rates. There is a chicken-and-egg problem involved in developing a sufficient degree of local autonomy so that a local currency can operate. This autonomy is exemplified in local barter exchanges, especially where the exchange is triangular, i.e., involves a credit system so that A can work for B, amassing credits (kept by a central record-keeping system) which he/she can then use to obtain needed goods or services from C. If, however, a significant slice of personal income must go toward the external purchase of cars, energy, or skills which must be imported, such a system of internal exchange cannot affect more than a fraction of total personal income available. Likewise, if a significant portion of local jobs are dependent on chains, subsidiaries, or franchises that are externally controlled, then neither will the earnings produced remain within the community, nor will the jobs created be paid in local currency.

A staged program of import substitution addressed to energy needs -- a major import of any community -- could start with electricity, as suggested in the preceding chapters, then move to heat use, and finally to transportation, probably the most difficult area for local substitution, requiring local production of ethanol or methanol, electric buses or street cars, and gas savings via group taxis and dial-a-buses. Financing could include municipal bonds, private investment with tax writeoffs and other deductions, and some arrangement with the state that would be able to capitalize the savings in welfare and unemployment resulting from local job creation. It might also be possible to begin to issue energy credits and transportation credits based on the future savings to the community, with the argument that not only would these credits, bought with dollars, be redeemable for energy or transportation. They would also result in a net saving to the community as a whole that would encompass both public and private sectors and individuals, thus offsetting the bond costs to the local government.

The virtue of a commodity-based currency where that commodity is widely used outside of the community -- kilowatt hours or lumber units are examples -- is that it provides a relatively stable basis for exchange that would allow for dollar redemption where external trade was involved. It might also encourage neighboring communities to accept local credits as well. However, a triangular bartering system that was supported not only by individuals but by local businesses could as easily be turned into a local currency simply by eliminating a central record-keeping system (which provides the Internal Revenue Service easy access to all transactions for tax purposes).

A labor credit system, without further support from a commodity-based currency, would be of use within a community so long as a significant level of personal expenses could be met with the use of these credits. Goods as well as services could probably be denominated in labor credits. The credit system could then be used to finance local projects at minimal cost, given the capacity to dictate interest rates locally. If housing mortgages were denominated in local currency, banks could offer low-cost mortgages, loans, and savings accounts, thus stimulating local building. However, for a local currency system to be acceptable on a regional basis, it would probably have to have the backing provided by a commodity base. Provided the commodity remained in fairly constant supply -- again lumber and kilowatt-hours are examples -- it would be proof against any internal tendencies toward inflation, and would therefore be attractive to users external to the community of origin.

For community members working outside the community and earning a dollar income, there would be a loss in converting to the community currency, assuming it was relatively inflation-proof as a result of a capacity to control internal inflation. Dollar values would lower the conversion rate, given continued external inflation. However, with the rationalization of internal transactions that both a local labor credit system and the removal of internal institutional and legal blocks would bring, there would be ample incentive to convert to the internal currency. The purchase of land, housing, and local commodities requiring financing would be attractive, given the fact that low finance costs would lower the price of these commodities. This in turn would create incentives to develop local sources of critical supplies. Locally available lumber for housing could be purchased in the local currency, thus avoiding a conversion loss, for example. A local currency would, once established, provide a strong impetus to develop even greater self-sufficiency.

We have seen that energy costs can be lowered by local substitutions. There are substitutions for major reliance on the private automobile and gasoline. The same holds true for land and housing, including finance costs. As for medical care, local health maintenance organizations can significantly lower costs by eliminating redundancy, using paraprofessionals, and substituting salaries for fees-for-service. For many communities, local food production is now, at a time of high transportation costs, an increasingly attractive option. It can be both rationalized and hastened by the development of a local warehousing and distribution system. The lack of such an infrastructure is the main reason communities have not moved in this direction already. (In Florida, the existence of a local distribution system helps keep food costs down.) With such a system in place, planning and incentives would be needed to create agricultural diversification, with local storage facilities able to lengthen the availability of local produce throughout the season.

Mobilizing a community around the goal of more effective overall resource utilization could be an effective method for achieving the necessary cohesiveness for making these kind of community-based financial arrangements work. This could be done by obtaining support on the part of local voluntary organizations, banks and other leading business institutions, and the county and municipal government for a conference on the subject.

Out of this would come a series of task forces focusing on energy substitution and conservation, transportation, housing, job creation, human services, food and agriculture, and medical care. The task forces would be made up of a mix of specialists in the area possessed of both the requisite knowledge and vision and representatives of interested local organizations.

Enough has been said to indicate that the approach being suggested here is able to avoid the zero-sum view which sees the enhancing of community services as being directly related to increased taxation. It is central to the self-financing idea that such financing represents an investment in the community future which will yield a return in lower costs and hence enhanced services for the same cost.  Equally, barter systems, energy and garbage cooperatives, and, with them, the other institutional replacements or alternatives suggested will reduce costs through greater efficiencies and thus also be self-financing.

The rationale for a local currency is that it is a logical further step in any such self-financing program.  Community support for such a program can be obtained if there is broad understanding that the program will, if anything, reduce (not raise) taxes, while significantly enhancing the local quality of life or, at least, preserving it from further degeneration.

In creating a local development and financing plan, the resource optimization approach leads to the idea of community mobilization, and this in turn contains presuppositions.  A pure conflict model will not allow community mobilization since this assumes alliances among citizens groups, mainstream voluntary organizations, businesses, and the local government in opposition to one another.  On the other hand, neither is a consensual view of community structure and community relations implied.  The assumption is rather that there is a fairly widespread and shared recognition of the failure of centralized institutions to respond to local needs and interests.

While the focus on resource optimization raises issues of external dependency, capital sources and costs, and legal and institutional obstacles to development, it also raises questions of allocation and distribution.  However, the issue is not how to divide up more equitably a static pie in zero-sum terms, but how to make more pie and then divide it more equitably.  And since this involves a program of community mobilization, majority interests can then be brought to bear on how to divide up the larger pie.

The present approach to local economic development leads to solutions different from the orthodox ones which typically involve creating industrial parks with tax breaks to lure outside businesses.  Local resource optimization leads naturally to such non-market mechanisms as barter, community development corporations, community investment funds, and cooperatives -- all of which combine an economic with a social function.  In the process, they eliminate the need to pay tribute to large centralized government and business systems.  They are also consumer- and local producer-oriented and can be community controlled.

# BIBLIOGRAPHY

*This bibliography is intended only to touch the high points of the literature on community economic change and the role of self-management and self-financing in that process.  But it does include a number of works that may properly be regarded as antecedents to some of the ideas, issues, and institutions discussed in this book, as well as a cross section of titles that have appeared more recently and that seek to build upon or extend these concepts.*

Anzalone, Joan, ed.  *Good Works:  A Guide to Careers in Social Change.*  3d ed.  New York:  Dembner Books, 1985.

Contains descriptions of some 450 organizations at the national, regional, and local level working for social change in the United States.  Included are a number concerned with community economic change.  Well-indexed by type of work and geographical location.  Preface by Ralph Nader.

Benello, C. George, and Dimitrios Roussopoulos, eds.  *The Case for Participatory Democracy.*  New York:  Viking Press, 1971.

A set of essays dealing with democratic group and organizational life, liberatory technology and work, strategies for change, and related topics.  Provides useful sociological background as well as some different perspectives on worker management.

Borsodi, Ralph.  *Seventeen Problems of Man and Society.*  London(?): Charotar Book Stall, 1968.

Borsodi's magnum opus.  One part, "The Possessional Problem," which provides the philosophical basis for the community land trust movement, was edited and revised by Gordon Lamuier and Lydia Ratcliff and published in the *Quest for Wisdom Series* of the International Independence Institute, Cambridge, Massachusetts, in 1968.  The 10-page essay is available from the Institute for Community Economics, 151 Montague City Road, Greenfield, MA 01301.

*177*

Brandow, Karen, and Jim McDonnell. *No Bosses Here: A Manual on Working Collectively and Cooperatively.* Boston: Alyson Publications, 1981.

A good manual on the organizational aspects of collectives and small cooperatives and how to make them work.

Brous, Ira, et al. *Democracy in the Workplace.* (Readings on the Implementation of Self-Management.) Washington, D.C.: Strongforce Series, 1977.

A manual for start-up of self-managed businesses, with sections on organizational development, education, legal, financial, and marketing issues. Knowledge in the field has advanced since this was written, but this is a good beginning.

Campbell, Keen, Norman, and Oakeshott. *Worker-Owners: The Mondragon Achievement.* London: Anglo-German Foundation for the Study of Industrial Society, 1978.

A short study of one of the most significant systems of worker cooperatives in Europe, and one of the major industrial complexes in Spain.

Cornuelle, Richard. *De-managing America: The Final Revolution.* New York: Vintage Books, 1977.

An imaginative essay by a former director of the National Association of Manufacturers, roundly criticizing current management styles and arguing for greater democratization of management.

Curl, John. *History of Work Cooperation in America.* Berkeley, California: Homeward Press, 1980.

A book about early American cooperatives and intentional communities up to the 1970s.

Ekins, Paul, ed. *The Living Economy: A New Economics in the Making.* New York: Routledge and Kegan Paul, 1987.

The book, which brings together some of the new economic ideas which surfaced during the 1970s, includes over 50 carefully edited papers and contributions from the 1984 and 1985 TOES (The Other Economic Summit) conferences in London and Bonn, spanning a wide range of economic activity and concerns.

Ellerman, David P. *The Socialization of Entrepreneurship: The Empresarial Division of the Caja Laboral Popular.* Somerville, Massachusetts: Industrial Cooperative Association, 1982.

A study of the Mondragon cooperatives with emphasis on the function of the  entrepreneurial division in the central bank of the Mondragon group of cooperatives.

_____. *What Is a Worker Cooperative?* Somerville, Massachusetts:  Industrial Cooperative Association, 1984.

A brief basic description, in question and answer form, of key aspects of worker cooperatives.

_____. *Worker Ownership: Economic Democracy or Worker Capitalism*. Somerville, Massachusetts:  Industrial Cooperative Association, 1986.

Discusses the two predominant models of worker ownership -- the capital-based, non-democratic, employee-owner corporation (e.g., conventional ESOPs) and the labor-based democratic form (e.g., a Mondragon-type worker cooperative or a democratic ESOP).

Ellerman, David P., and Peter Pitegoff. "The Democratic Corporation: The New Worker Cooperative Statute in Massachusetts." *New York University Review of Law and Social Change* 11, No. 3 (1982-1983): 441-472.

Describes the origins and main features of and rational for the worker cooperative corporation law enacted in Massachusetts in 1982 (and subsequently in several other states). A worker cooperative created under this law would generally follow the Mondragon model. Also includes the text of the Massachusetts statute.

*The Employee Ownership Report*. National Center for Employee Ownership, Suite 650, 426 17th Street, Oakland, CA  94612.

A bimonthly bulletin of current information on legal, tax, legislative, and other developments affecting ESOPs.

French, David, and Elena French. *Working Communally:  Patterns and Possibilities*. New York:  Russell Sage Foundation, 1975.

Communally oriented work communities in the United States, from the first experiments through to the mid-1970s.

George, Henry. *Progress and Poverty:  An Inquiry into the Cause of Industrial Responsibility and of Increase of Want with Increase of Wealth; the Remedy*. New York:  Robert Schalkenback, 1979.

This classic analyzes the problem of the unearned increment in land values and its impact on society and sets forth the author's famous "Single Tax" method for dealing with it.

Hayek, Frederick A. *Denationalisation of Money*. 2d ed. (Hobart Paper No. 70). London: Transatlantic Arts, 1977.

A basic work on problems with the existing monetary system and how they can be overcome. (Available from Trans-Atlantic, P.O. Box 6086, Albuquerque, NM 87197.)

Honigsberg, Peter Jan, Bernard Kamaroff, and Jim Beatty. *We Own It: Starting and Managing Coops, Collectives & Employee Owned Enterprises*. Laytonville, California: Bell Springs, 1982.

This handbook provides legal, tax, management, and other basic information on cooperatives of various types -- consumer and producer, worker-owned, collective. It also covers different legal entities, including non-profit, for profit, and cooperative corporations, and contains a listing of each state's legal requirements.

Industrial Cooperative Association. *ICA Model By-Laws for a Workers' Cooperative (Version 2)*. Somerville, Massachusetts: ICA, 1983.

This looseleaf includes model by-laws for a workers' cooperative with a Mondragon-type legal structure, along with detailed annotations, explanations, and model forms. The purchase price includes an hour of free consulting time from ICA (Suite 203, 58 Day Street, Somerville, MA 02144).

Institute for Community Economics. *The Community Land Trust Handbook*. Emmaus, Pennsylvania: Rodale Press, 1982.

Provides a series of case studies of Community Land Trusts in different parts of the United States. It also includes a practical guide on how to create a Community Land Trust, covering such matters as financing, land acquisition, and legal arrangements with leaseholders. (The *Handbook* is available directly from ICE, 151 Montague City Road, Greenfield, MA 01301.)

_____. *The Community Loan Fund Manual*. Greenfield, Massachusetts: ICE, 1987.

In a looseleaf format, this manual includes a model of a community loan fund, a practical guide to starting and managing such a fund, and case studies of three actual funds.

Kamaroff, Bernard. *Small Time Operator: How to Start Your Own Small Business, Keep Your Books, Pay Your Taxes, & Stay Out of Trouble -- A Guide and Workbook*. Laytonville, California: Bell Springs, 1986.

A how-to-do-it handbook for small businesses. Describes legal and tax problems, other government regulations, personnel procedures, and other practical issues facing the small business. Also includes a section on the fundamentals of bookkeeping and financial management.

Kelso, Louis O. *The Capitalist Manifesto*. New York: Random House, 1958.

Kelso, Louis O., and Mortimer J. Adler. *The New Capitalists: A Proposal to Free Economic Growth from the Slavery of Savings*. New York: Random House, 1981.

Kelso, Louis O., and Patricia Hetter. *The Two Factor Theory -- The Economics of Reality*. New York: Vintage Books, 1967.

These three works are by (with co-authors) one of the prime movers behind the most widely practiced method of redistributing ownership of productive assets to workers in North America, the Employee Stock Ownership Plan. They set forth the underlying rationale for his advocacy of ESOPs and other structural changes in the capitalist system.

Likert, Rensis. *New Patterns of Management*. New York: McGraw-Hill, 1961.

A basic work of the new, participatory management school with a useful structural emphasis.

Lindenfield, Frank, and Joyce Rothschild-Whitt, eds. *Workplace Democracy and Social Change*. Boston: Porter Sargent, 1982.

A useful collection of essays, exploring the relationship between democracy in the workplace and broader aspects of social change. Includes a chapter by C. George Benello.

Linton, Michael, comp. LETS (Local Exchange Trading System) Information Package. Courtenay, British Columbia: Landsman Community Services, n.d.

The package includes printed materials, LETSplay game materials, graphics, and three computer diskettes with over 220 pages of text and 50 pages of program codes for running the LETSystem accounting and notice programs. Contact LCS, 375 Johnston Avenue, Courtenay, B.C. V9N 2Y2, Canada.

Lutz, Mark A., and Kenneth Lux. *Humanistic Economics: The New Challenge*. New York: The Bootstrap Press, 1988.

A major new work in social economics, carrying forward E.F. Schumacher's tradition of "economics as if people mattered." After a penetrating critique of conventional economics, the authors make a systematic presentation of an alternative economics based on the satisfaction of human needs and drawing extensively on the insights of social psychology.

McGregor, Douglas. *The Human Side of Enterprise*. New York: McGraw-Hill, 1960.

One of the most important books laying the groundwork for modern participatory management, which uses Maslow's hierarchy of needs as the basis for a new theory of worker motivation.

McRobie, George. *Small is Possible*. New York: Harper and Row, 1981.

The third book in the planned trilogy shows who is doing what to create lifestyles and technologies on a human scale, focusing on the activities of the Intermediate Technology Development Group and counterpart organizations in Africa, India, and Latin America. A chapter is devoted to the three developed countries of Canada, the United States, and the United Kingdom.

National Association of Community Development Loan Funds. *National Association of Community Development Loan Funds Directory of Members*. Greenfield, Massachusetts: Institute for Community Economics, 1989.

Profiles some 30 community development loan fund members of NACDLF. A useful resource for those seeking alternative financing for community-based economic initiatives, ranging from low-income housing and preservation of natural resources to ethically and environmentally sound small businesses.

Oakeshott, Robert. *The Case for Worker's Coops*. London: Routledge and Kegan Paul, 1978.

A basic study of worker cooperatives. Includes a detailed examination of the Mondragon experiment.

Phillips, Michael, and Salli Rasberry. *Honest Business: A Superior Strategy for Starting and Managing Your Own Business*. New York: Random House, 1981.

This classic, based on the authors' experience with over 450 businesses, provides a guide to a business strategy that emphasizes openness, community service, and extensive access to information. The authors show how starting with less money -- rather than more -- is a good business practice.

Pitegoff, Peter. *The Democratic ESOP*. Somerville, Massachusetts: Industrial Cooperative Association, 1987.

An introduction to employee stock ownership plans (ESOPs) and their potential use in building democratic worker-owned corporations.

Ross, David P., and Peter J. Usher. *From the Roots Up: Economic Development as if Community Mattered*. New York: The Bootstrap Press, 1986.

A major work on the informal economy and its role in building sustainable communities in North America. The book analyzes the changing relationship between household and community economic systems, based on how the "hidden economy" really works in the U.S., Canada, and other industrialized countries.

Sale, Kirkpatrick. *Dwellers in the Land: The Bioregional Vision*. New York: Random House, 1985.

A comprehensive and authoritative account of the bioregional movement in North America, with its insistence on an ecological orientation in the way we organize our communities and our daily lives.

_____. *Human Scale*. New York: Coward, McCann, and Geoghegan, 1980.

A comprehensive examination of the dangers of continuing the concentration of economic activity fueled by the preoccupation with maintaining rapid resource-depleting, environmentally destructive growth. Provides concrete examples of ways to scale down economic, social, and political institutions to provide better housing, food production, waste disposal, transportation, heath care, and schools.

Schaaf, Michael. *Cooperatives at the Crossroads: The Potential for a Major New Economic and Social Role*. Washington, D.C.: Exploratory Project for Economic Alternatives, 1977.

A useful book about cooperatives of all varieties, with cases taken from the United States and a study of the cooperative movement in Sweden. It locates worker cooperatives within a broader context of consumer, housing, and producer cooperatives.

Schumacher, E.F. *Small is Beautiful: Economics as if People Mattered*. New York: Harper and Row, 1973.

This classic calls for an economics that is subordinated to human scale and human needs.  Contains an essay, "Buddhist Economics," which stands the conventional economic assumptions on their head.

_____. *Good Work*.  New York:  Harper and Row, 1980.

Compiled mainly from a series of lectures Schumacher gave in the United States during the mid-1970s, this book explores the political, managerial, social, and economic consequences of conventional technology and values -- and of the more sustainable, emerging alternatives.  The three purposes of human work are identified as producing necessary and useful goods and services, enabling us to use and perfect personal gifts and skills, and serving and collaborating with others.

Shankland, Graeme.  *Wonted Work:  A Guide to the Informal Economy*.  New York:  The Bootstrap Press, 1988.

A pioneering study on the informal economy, drawing primarily on the British experience but with findings and insights applicable to Canada, the United States, and other post-industrial societies.  The author examines the relationship between the informal and formal economies and major components of the former.

Speiser, Stuart M.  *Mainstreet Capitalism:  Essays on Broadening Share Ownership in America and Britain*.  New York:  New Horizons Press, 1988.

The contributors to this volume address the question of how the fruits of capitalism can be more equitably distributed by examining economic and political obstacles to broadening share ownership and by proposing alternative ways of achieving economic justice in the British and American capitalist systems.  Included are the winning essays in contests on Universal Capitalism held in each country in 1986.

_____. *The USOP Handbook:  A Guide to Designing Universal Share Ownership Plans for the United States and Great Britain*.  New York:  Council on International and Public Affairs, 1986.

Examines alternative plans to broadening ownership of productive assets and addresses some of the practical questions that need to be addressed in working toward implementation of such plans.

Steiner, Rudolf.  *World Economy*.  3d ed.  London:  Anthroposophic Press, 1972.

Another classic by an innovative social and economic thinker.  Explores the role that control of natural and productive resources plays in the global political economy. (Available from Anthroposophic at Bell's Pond, Star Route, Hudson, NY 12534.)

Swann, Robert. "The Community Land Trust: An Alternative." *Whole Earth Papers*, No. 17. East Orange, New Jersey: Global Education Associates, April 1982.

Relatively little has been published on Community Land Trusts. This article provides a useful overview in published form. (GEA is now located at 475 Riverside Drive, New York, NY 10115.)

Thayer, Frederick. *An End to Hierarchy, an End to Competition*. 2d ed. New York: Franklin Watts, 1981.

An imaginative critique of bureaucracy with a suggestion for organizational alternatives by someone who has been called "an organizational romantic." This book nevertheless serves as a landmark in administrative theory.

Thomas, H., and C. Logan. *Mondragon: An Economic Analysis*. London: George Allen and Unwin, 1982.

An authoritative study of the largest group of worker cooperatives in the world located in the Basque region of Spain.

Turnbull, Shann. *Democratising the Wealth of Nations*. Sydney: Company Directors Association of Australia, 1975.

In this basic work, the author builds upon Louis Kelso's pioneering initiatives by complementing the Employee Stock Ownership Plan (ESOP) with his own proposals for sharing wealth through the Ownership Transfer Corporation (OTC), Cooperative Land Bank (CLB), and Producer-Consumer Cooperative (PCC). All four provide the building blocks of "social capitalism."

_____. "Beyond Federalism -- Self-Financing Local Government." *Royal Australian Planning Institute Journal* 17, No. 1 (February 1979).

_____. "Co-operative Land Banks for Low-Income Housing." In Schlomo Angel and R.W. Archer, eds. *Land for Housing the Poor*. Singapore: Select Books, 1983.

_____. "Time Limited Corporations." *Abacus* 9, No. 1 (June 1973).

The above three entries amplify the two basic ideas of the author presented in the book -- Cooperative Land Banks and Ownership

Transfer Corporations (which he earlier labeled "Time Limited Corporations").

Vanek, Jaroslav, ed. *Self-Management, Economic Liberation of Man.* New York: Penguin Books, 1975.

A useful reader, including sections on doctrine, case studies, performance, and economic theory. The introduction by Vanek represents a good introductory essay on worker management.

Whyte, William Foote, and Kathleen King Whyte. *Making Mondragon: The Growth and Dynamics of the Worker Cooperative Complex.* (Cornell International and Labor Relations Report No. 14.) Ithaca: ILR Press, Cornell University, 1988.

A comprehensive and authoritative account of a remarkable social initiative in building a network of highly successful worker cooperatives and supporting institutions. Widely regarded as a landmark study in English.

Wisman, Jon. "Economic Reform for Humanity's Greatest Struggle." New York: Council on International and Public Affairs, 1986.

The prize-winning entry in the 1984-85 Speiser Essay Contest. Advocates widespread worker ownership of the means of production -- i.e., their own tools -- as the only way to remain competitive in an increasingly competitive global economy and to adapt to the labor-displacing potential of modern technology. (Published in Kenneth B. Taylor, ed. *Capitalism and the 'Evil Empire': Reducing Superpower Conflict Through American Economic Reform.* New York: New Horizons Press, 1988.)

*Worker Co-ops.* Centre for the Study of Cooperatives, University of Saskatchewan, Saskatoon, Saskatchewan S7N 0W0, Canada.

An independent quarterly magazine published by the Worker Ownership Development Foundation in Toronto, the Centre for the Study of Cooperatives in Saskatchewan, and other Canadian groups. Provides extensive information on new developments affecting worker cooperatives. While the orientation is Canadian, the coverage is international. The most comprehensive single source of current information available.

Zwerdling, Daniel. *Workplace Democracy: A Guide to Workplace Experiments in the United States and Europe.* New York: Harper and Row, 1980.

A useful series of case studies primarily from the United States, but also including chapters on Mondragon in Spain and on worker-owned companies in Yugoslavia. The case studies include both Quality of Work Life experiments as well as fully self-managed enterprises and cooperatives. Invaluable as a text for an introductory course in self-management.